TELLING THE TALE

The African-American Fiction Writer's Guide

ANGELA BENSON

D0094650

BERKLEY BOOKS, NEW YORK

This is an original publication of
The Berkley Publishing Group.

TELLING THE TALE:
THE AFRICAN-AMERICAN FICTION WRITER'S GUIDE

A Berkley Book / published by arrangement with
the author

PRINTING HISTORY
Berkley trade paperback edition / May 2000

All rights reserved.
Copyright © 2000 by Angela Benson.
Book design by Tiffany Kukec.
Cover design by Karen Katz.
This book may not be reproduced in whole or in part,
by mimeograph or any other means, without permission.
For information address: The Berkley Publishing Group, a division of
Penguin Putnam Inc., 375 Hudson Street, New York, New York 10014.

The Penguin Putnam Inc. World Wide Web site address is
http://www.penguinputnam.com

ISBN: 0-425-17054-3

BERKLEY®
Berkley Books are published by The Berkley Publishing Group,
a division of Penguin Putnam Inc., 375 Hudson Street, New York,
New York 10014.
BERKLEY and the "B" design
are trademarks belonging to Penguin Putnam Inc.

PRINTED IN THE UNITED STATES OF AMERICA

10 9 8 7 6 5 4 3 2 1

CONTENTS

INTRODUCTION

〰〰〰〰〰〰〰〰〰〰〰〰〰〰〰〰〰〰

When I finished that book [Toni Morrison's The Bluest Eye*], I had all the permission I needed to become a writer. Someone who looked like me had written a masterpiece.*

—Bebe Moore Campbell
(author of *Singing in the Comeback Choir*),
Time magazine, 1996

A WRITER'S TALE

Oftentimes people ask me how I started writing. And it's always a difficult question for me to answer because I never know where to start. Do I start in 1970 when I wrote my first story in Ms. Milazo's fifth grade class or do I start in 1992 when I attended the Romantic Times Readers and Writers Convention in Savannah, Georgia? For this introduction, I think it appropriate that I start in 1992.

Prior to 1992, I was a research engineer for a major telecommunications company. My job was planning new telephone services. I used to tell people that it was the best job in the world—if you had to work for a living. And it was true. It was a wonderful job. But sometime around 1990 I began to go through what I now call an early midlife crisis. I began to question my job and the role it played in my life. Was my job something I did or was it an extension of who I was as an individual? The unsettling and unsatisfying answer was that my job was something I did that was completely separate from who I was as a person. On some level this separation could be considered a good thing, but my reasoning was that if I was going to spend *at least* one-third of every day of my life working at something, it should be something that was an extension of who I was as a person. A lofty goal, I admit, but that lofty goal set me off on a quest to find a vocation that would fulfill my financial needs as well as my personal need for self-expression.

The journey took me down several paths. I sold Amway for about two weeks, until I realized that I didn't like being away from home so much of the time. I investigated becoming a secondary school teacher and would have done so had I not been told that first I had to take a computer science course. Taking a computer course seemed redundant, given that I'd been working as an engineer for over ten years. Next, I became a distributor for a multilevel marketing diet program thinking that I could lose weight then help others to lose weight too. That brief stint ended when I realized I wasn't losing any weight. I could go on, but I think you get the point: I made a lot of false starts in my quest for a new and fulfilling vocation.

I finally hit the motherlode in 1992 while on a business trip in New Jersey. A closet romance reader since my college days, I ran across a copy of *Romantic Times* magazine in a local bookstore and learned about the Readers and Writers Convention being held that weekend in Savannah, not far from my Atlanta home. After checking with the airlines and learning that a round-trip ticket to Savannah would add only one hundred dollars to my fare, I decided to attend the convention.

That decision changed my life. Sounds dramatic, I know, but it's true. Writing workshops given by published authors were a part of the convention agenda. One of the workshops I attended was conducted by three romance writers who'd each had more than one book published. I don't remember the topic or anything specific that the authors said, but I do remember that as they spoke, a single thought formed in my mind: *They don't look any smarter than me. If they can write a book, so can I.*

And so began my writing career. I went back home, joined a local writers' group, and began my first novel. That novel, which I started in early 1992, was completed in early 1993, sold to Pinnacle Books in late 1993, and arrived in bookstores in late 1994.

Some of my published friends hate it when I tell this story. They accuse me of perpetuating the myth that anybody with a pencil (or a typewriter or a computer) can write a book. They say that the story, especially my epiphany, completely discounts the skills that a writer must cultivate in order to produce a publishable book. I agree with them to a point, but I continue to tell the story for three reasons.

First, the story shows that I came to writing because I had a need to express myself more fully. I didn't start writing for the big-money payoff; I started writing because there was something inside me that I wanted and needed to explore.

Second, the story shows that I had some faith in my ability to become a writer. In my mind, becoming a writer was an attainable goal. Like most endeavors, though, writing required a lot more work than I had expected and with it came more disappointment than I could have imagined. Fortunately, the childlike faith that motivated me to start has kept me writing in spite of the disappointments.

Third, the story shows the power of living and breathing examples. I decided I could become a writer because I saw other people not that much different from myself (at least, I didn't focus on the differences) who had become writers. The women who gave that workshop at the convention were giving hope as much as they were teaching writing skills.

The third point is the reason I decided to write *Telling the*

Tale. This book is my way of serving as a living and breathing example to you and other would-be and novice writers I will probably never have the opportunity to meet. I hope that as you read this book and complete the assignments your faith in your ability to *tell your own tale* will be enhanced. I want you to read this book and think as I thought back in 1992: *She doesn't seem any smarter than me. If she can write a book, so can I.*

TELLING YOUR TALE

I wrote *Telling the Tale* to help you complete your novel and hone your writing skills. In order to make the most effective use of this book you need to understand its three main characteristics.

First, *Telling the Tale* surveys the broad spectrum of technical writing skills needed to produce a well-crafted novel and provides references for more detailed study. The topics covered range from voice and point of view to plotting and characterization to research and revision.

Second, the exercises provided in *Telling the Tale* are designed for easy application to your current work-in-progress, thereby allowing you to improve your writing skills while completing your current writing project or starting a new one. The key to success with *Telling the Tale* is completing the exercises. You don't learn to write by reading about writing; you learn to write by writing. I cannot stress this point enough: You must complete the exercises if you want to obtain the maximum benefit from this book. Some of the exercises will be fun for you, while others may seem like torture. But guess what? Sometimes writing is fun, and sometimes it's torture. You'll have to learn to write through those torturous times, and you can start by committing yourself to working through the exercises in this book.

Third, while the writing fundamentals presented in this book are universal and appropriate for all new and beginning writers, *Telling the Tale* embraces and reflects the black perspective through the liberal use of familiar examples from successful black books, television shows, and movies. In addition to illustrating the concepts presented, the examples serve as a reminder of the success of blacks in the arts—success that will inspire and encourage you as you pursue your writing goals.

ONE

BEING A WRITER MEANS WRITING

~~~~~~

The one thing I would say, and I say it often, is just sit down and write. Don't get frustrated. Don't give up. Now when I look back, I realize that all those false starts and decisions to give up were not wasted time and energy. It was a process I was going through in teaching myself how to be a writer. If you want to be a writer, you have to practice writing. You have to sit at the typewriter day after day, even when it doesn't sound the way you want it to sound. Even if it feels as if nothing is happening, on some level something is. My advice would be, just write!

—Connie Briscoe
(author of *A Long Way from Home*),
Quarterly Black Review, 1997

OVERNIGHT SUCCESS STORIES
Some Nights Are Longer Than Others

Million-dollar book contracts, movie projects with Denzel and Wesley, interviews on *Oprah*. All these and more will be yours as soon as you finish the masterpiece of romance, intrigue, and plain-old-brilliance that's rolling around in your head.

Are those thoughts familiar? Well, dreams are what make the world go 'round. So keep dreaming and keep working toward making your dreams come true. Just to add a touch of reality to your dreams, though, let's take a brief look at the careers of some well-known, and some not-so-well-known, authors. As you read their stories, think about yourself, where you are in your writing career, and where you want to be a few years down the road.

Terry McMillan

Many people view Terry McMillan (*How Stella Got Her Groove Back*) as an overnight success. They say they want careers like hers, but what they really want is her success, not the hard work and long years that went into creating it. Terry, who has an undergraduate degree in journalism and who has been writing since her college days, saw her first book, *Mama*, published in 1987. While the critics loved it, neither *Mama* nor her next book, *Disappearing Acts*, brought her anywhere near the success she attained with the 1992 *New York Times* bestseller *Waiting to Exhale*.

E. Lynn Harris

Discontent in his career in computer sales, Lynn Harris (*Abide with Me*) quit his job in 1990 and wrote his first book, *Invisible Life*. After it was rejected by every New York publisher he sent it to, Harris depleted his personal savings account to publish the book himself. Then he sold it out of the trunk of his car. I've heard him tell the story of going to reading groups and having to look successful when in reality he needed the money from his book sales that night to pay for his next meal. He rose to fame after Doubleday bought the rights to *Invisible Life* in 1992. He first appeared on the *New York Times* bestseller list in 1996 with his third book, *And This Too Shall Pass*.

Walter Mosley

Another overnight success, right? Wrong. Looking for personal fulfillment, ex–computer programmer Walter Mosley (*Blue Light*) started writing in the mid-1980s. His first book, *Gone Fishin'* (Black Classic Press, 1997), was rejected by every major publisher the first time around. His second book, *Devil in a Blue Dress* (W. W. Norton, 1990), became his first published work. He rose to success in 1992 after then–presidential candidate Bill Clinton revealed to the nation—the world even—that Walter Mosley was his favorite mystery writer.

Evelyn Coleman

Evelyn Coleman, the author of six children's books, saw her first adult title, *What a Woman's Gotta Do*, published in hardcover by Simon and Schuster in 1998. Before publishing her children's books, Evelyn spent ten years learning the craft of writing. One summer she read, studied, and dissected over 500 picture books and spent $6,000 on writing classes. It's pretty clear that Evelyn's "overnight" success took a long, long time and a lot of hard work.

Nora DeLoach

Nora DeLoach (*Mama Rocks the Empty Cradle*), whose writing career began in 1991, sold five paperback books to a small, independent publisher, Holloway House, before signing a four-book hardcover deal with Bantam Doubleday Dell in 1996. Her first Bantam title, *Mama Stalks the Past*, was published in 1997.

Lolita Files

It took former KinderCare manager Lolita Files (*Getting to the Good Part*) only fifteen hours to acquire an agent, making her a true overnight success, right? Wrong. Ms. Files's successful debut work, *Scenes from a Sistah*, was actually the second book she wrote. The first was completed more than a year before she wrote *Scenes*.

Reviewing the career paths of multiply published authors can help us keep our feet grounded in reality even as our dreams soar into the stratosphere. Terry McMillan, Walter Mosley, and E. Lynn Harris have reached a level of success that few authors attain. Terry's success came after years of writing. Walter Mosley's success was accelerated by the endorsement of a presidential candidate. Lynn Harris made great short-term sacrifices in order to achieve his success, and his marketing savvy was a definite plus. Have you been writing as long as Terry? Can you count on a national figure endorsing your book? Do you have the freedom to quit your job, or the marketing savvy to publish your work yourself and then sell it out of the trunk of your car?

Evelyn Coleman, Nora DeLoach, and Lolita Files are less well known authors who are building successful writing careers. Evelyn invested time and money into honing her craft. Nora paid her dues at a small publisher before joining the ranks of a major publishing house. Lolita, who had great success in finding an agent, didn't sell the first book she wrote. Though these three authors have achieved nowhere near the success of the McMillans, Mosleys, and Harrises of the world, they serve as examples for us to follow. Follow Evelyn's lead and do what it takes to learn your craft. Let Nora's footsteps lead you to consider alternatives to the mighty New York publishers. And, like Lolita, don't stop writing if your first book goes unpublished.

EXERCISE 1

You have to define success for yourself. My only advice is not to let your success be defined by forces beyond your control. The following questions will help you think through success and what it means to you and your writing career.

1.1. What criteria do you use to measure success? Why do you use those criteria?

1.2. List your three favorite authors. Find out when they started writing, the number of books they wrote before they sold their first story, and at least one anecdote about how they overcame adversity in their career. Start with back issues of popular magazines like *Ebony* and *Essence*, and major newspapers. Your local library has indexes that can help you locate the information you need.

1.3. Review what you've learned about your favorite authors. How successful do you consider them to be?

1.4. What expectations do you have for your writing future? Do you think those expectations are realistic? What are you doing to enhance your chances for success?

THE WRITER'S VOICE

The essence of being a writer is writing, that solitary and sometimes lonely endeavor that occurs between you and whatever instrument you use to put words on paper. Writing is what happens late at night, or early in the morning, or around midday, whatever time of day the story idea that was birthed in your head comes to life on paper or on a computer screen. Simply put, writing is you making a record of your story.

Writing is not selling your book. Writing is not a six-figure paycheck with your name on it. Writing is not book tours with hundreds of screaming fans waiting, book in hand, for your autograph. These are events that *could* happen in a writer's life but they are not to be confused with the writing process. Selling your book comes *after* you've written it. Paychecks, both the six-figure kind and those for much less, come *after* you've written and sold your book. Book tours, if they happen at all, come *after* the book you've written and sold has been published.

Some writers say that they don't like writing, but they like having written. In other words, they like being finished with a work. I find joy in the writing process. Of course, there are times when the process is a struggle. Sometimes it's torture. But even during the toughest times I still find enjoyment. Maybe that's because writing, for me, is a test of wits with myself, the ultimate mind game. Can I pull off this story? Can I make these characters come alive? Can I tell this story in such a way that some reader on the other side of the country, the other side of world even, will discover its riches?

But writing is more than an internal battle of wits. Writing is also the ultimate test of my willingness to expose myself, my beliefs, and my views to the world. Though I have never been a character in one of my books, all of my books have been about me. The essence of each story idea and the way that story idea is executed reveals something about me— whether I deliberately set out to reveal myself or not.

As a writer, your basic philosophies of life play themselves out in the battles—physical and emotional—of your characters. This is what I call your *voice* in action. Voice is the *you* that you bring to your story. It's your perspective on the world, or at least that part of the world in which you've chosen to place your characters.

For an introduction to this concept of voice, let's take a look at the music industry. It's pretty obvious that we'll find all sorts of voices here, and I'm not just talking tonal quality. Sure, Babyface's voice is different from Barry White's voice. We hear the grittiness of Barry White versus the soft, melodic strands of Babyface. But *voice* goes beyond the tonal differences. It encompasses everything from lyrics to CD packaging.

Have you ever bought a music CD before hearing a single track? Sure you have. Music buyers often buy a new release because they like the artist's previous work. You've probably heard someone say, "I love that Babyface sound." And if you've ever heard a Babyface song, I bet you knew exactly the sound they were talking about. Babyface talks about love and relationships much differently from how Luther Vandross, Barry White, R. Kelley, or BeBe and CeCe Winans do. Some people love Babyface but they hate R. Kelley. Some people love BeBe and CeCe but they hate Barry White. Why this difference in listening preference when all of the artists sing well and they all sing about love and relationships? One reason is that each brings a unique perspective to his or her songs of love.

Babyface's songs celebrate and praise women. They are about men who can be counted on, even when their women seem undeserving of their loyalty. Barry White tends to be more overtly sexual. While Babyface sings about emotional satisfaction, Barry tends to address physical satisfaction. BeBe and CeCe bring a spiritual perspective to their work. They sing of love and relationships within the context of God's love for His creation. Three different approaches to the topic of love and relationships. And all three approaches have found phenomenal success.

This same notion of voice can be applied to books. Think about Terry McMillan and Tina McElroy Ansa. Both women write contemporary stories about women and relationships.

Terry does it with a quick, urban flavor that revitalized the genre of contemporary African American fiction. Terry tells an in-your-face kind of story and, from what I've seen of her, I think I can safely say that she's an in-your-face kind of woman who views in-your-face-ness as a positive character trait. That's why you see the trait in her characters. Tina's message is a bit more subtle, but no less powerful. It's as though her characters hide themselves from the reader, forcing the reader to sift through details of the story to discover each character's true identity. While some readers enjoy both Tina's and Terry's stories, I would guess that many readers prefer one over the other.

Voice comes out of who we are as people—as mothers, fathers, brothers, sisters, friends, enemies, lovers, employers, employees, you name it. We bring our unique perspective on those experiences with us when we sit down to write and it is through that perspective that we tell our story. The stories you choose to write and the audience you choose to write for are a product of your voice. You write about topics that are interesting or important to you and topics that you hope will be interesting to your readers.

It's easiest to see how voices vary when several writers are given the same premise and asked to create a story. Say, for example, three writers are asked to create a story about a divorced man who remarries three years after his first marriage ended. One writer might focus on the bitterness of the first marriage that carries over into the second marriage. Another might address the beauty of second chances. The third might delve into the effects of the new relationship on the children of the first marriage. As you can see, there are many angles from which to tackle a story idea and your voice is a big factor in determining which angle you choose.

Voice is the most powerful and potent resource that you bring to the writing process. Unfortunately, many factors work against the writer achieving and maintaining a unique voice. One factor is the desire to be published. Writers desperate to be published try to write what they think will sell. In the process some lose their voice. Instead of writing from their own perspective, they try to adopt someone else's. We all hope for success like Terry McMillan's or E. Lynn Harris's or Walter Mosley's, but slavishly aping their work isn't a formula for success.

I started writing after the success of *Waiting to Exhale*, so I was among the many would-be writers with dreams of grandeur. My first attempt was a story about four women friends who had various problems with men. Sound familiar? I was trying, though not consciously, to write a Terry McMillan story. Of course, I could only copy her so far. Since my mind doesn't work like hers, my characters were nowhere near as over-the-top as *Waiting to Exhale*'s Bernadine, Savannah, Gloria, and Robin. My story was dry and lifeless. I wanted so much to have Terry's success that I tried to tell Terry's story. Guess what? It didn't work.

The desperate-to-be-published writer is also susceptible to the "genre formula, get-published-quickly" syndrome. I wrote what the book publishing industry terms romance fiction, and now I write Christian romance fiction. Romance fiction falls under the banner of genre fiction. Mysteries, science fiction, westerns, and fantasy are also considered genre fiction. Genre fiction usually has guidelines defining what readers and publishers expect in books of that type. The challenge to writing genre fiction is to write within the guidelines while at the same time maintaining your own voice, a task that many writers find impossible.

My first two romance novels probably had more of my voice than the third and fourth because the first two were written before I made my first sale. As I learned more about the romance genre, I found myself trying to conform more to the genre guidelines. Bad move. Fortunately, by the time I wrote book number five I recognized the importance of my voice. During this period, my voice was moving away from traditional genre romance and toward the more inspirational and Christian-themed stories. Instead of ignoring the shift or fighting against it, I switched to writing the Christian-themed romances. Instead of forcing my voice to fit genre guidelines, I looked for a genre that could accommodate my changing voice.

This is a path I recommend. Instead of finding out what publishers are buying or trying to figure out what the next fiction trend is going to be, I suggest you write your story in your voice and then decide where it fits. Conventional wisdom says taking this path will result in your taking longer to sell your book. This may be true, but so what? You're a writer and you're going to be writing for a very long time. Your best bet is to write what's inside you rather than to re-create what's already on the bookshelves. It took me eight books to realize that writing outside my voice was distinctly unsatisfying.

The second factor working against the writer maintaining her voice is fear. Yes, fear. Fear of self-exposure. I'm not talking about exposure in the sense that people will know your story contains incidents from your life, but exposure in the sense that your story deals with issues that have personal significance for you. My first book is not my most well written work in the technical sense, but while writing that book I came face-to-face with my voice. At one point, I felt so close to the story that I had to go back and change the plot so that the story wouldn't contain so much of me. The heroine in my first book had never known her father. I grew up much the same way (which is probably why I made it a part of my heroine's background), and I found it difficult to delve into the issues facing a woman who grew up without her natural father. The issue was much too close to me so I backed off. My story ended with the heroine reunited with a loving father. No doubt my voice—the way I wanted the world to be—played a significant role in my choice of ending.

Other writers have different experiences with voice. One writer I know worked through the issues of her mother's death while writing a romance novel. Nobody in her book died, but the deep emotional responses of her characters mirrored the author's grief over the death of her mother. As a writer, you will find yourself using emotions stirred up by events in your life to help you chart the emotional paths of your characters.

Thriller writer Evelyn Coleman creates strong-willed, street-talking female characters who embody many of the characteristics that I see in her, but who are very different in temperament and personality from the soft-spoken Evelyn. Evelyn's characters are created out of who she is, but her characters are not her. Likewise, your characters are not you, but you create them, so most likely you will see some of yourself in them.

A third factor that works against a writer maintaining her voice is the changing nature of voice. Change is natural. You should expect your writing to mature as you mature, and your voice to change as you change. Instead of working to keep your voice the same, your goal should be to know your voice and to follow where it leads without fear. I'm still learning to trust my voice, to not pull back from it, but to allow it to emerge.

While voice is not a complicated concept, many new writers find it difficult to grasp. I was one of them. If you're like me, don't fret; the concept will become clearer as you complete the following exercises.

EXERCISE 2

2.1. Go to the mall or the park or any place where you can observe people in action. Take a pad and pencil and a friend with you. A writer friend would be good, but any friend will do. Your assignment is to observe and record. Pick a person or a storefront or a sign and spend five minutes writing a description of it. Be sure to use all your senses as you write your description. Write what you see and what you don't see. Write what you feel, both physically and emotionally. Write the sounds you hear and the thoughts you think as you observe. When the five minutes are up, focus on something else. Continue this assignment for at least an hour. When you're done, compare notes with your friend. Talk about the differences and similarities in your observations. When you complete this exercise, you should have some clear examples of how voice determines what you see, how you see it, and how you choose to describe it.

2.2. Your voice influences your reading preferences. The following exercises will demonstrate that influence.

2.2.1. List the last ten novels you've read.

2.2.2. Why did you read these books?

2.2.3. What did you like best about them?

2.2.4. What did you like least about them?

2.2.5. If you could rewrite the stories, what, if anything, would you change in them? Why would you make these changes?

NOT ENOUGH HOURS IN THE DAY

The person who *wants to write* can come up with a million excuses why she doesn't write. Near the top of the list will be time—not enough of it. The person who *writes* finds or makes the time to write because writing is important to her.

When I started writing, my major problem was finding time. I was working full-time at a very demanding job and I didn't have the energy to write when I came home after a hard day's work. Well, that's the excuse I used. But after I committed myself to writing and completing my first book, I found time. I decided to write on weekends. Yes, weekends. I forced myself to write on Saturday mornings before doing my errands. My goal was to write one chapter before leaving the house. Since my chapters tended to be around fifteen pages long, one chapter was a reasonable goal.

Being a member of a critique group also helped to keep me on track. My critique group consisted of four writers who met on a regular basis, usually weekly, to critique our work and encourage one another. Knowing that I was going to meet with the group on Monday nights motivated me to write on weekends. I did not want to show up at those meetings empty-handed. Though I did most of my actual writing on weekends, I used weeknights to edit what I'd written, to study books on the writing craft, and to review and edit the work of my critique partners.

A weekend writing schedule worked for me and my lifestyle, though I have to confess that I didn't write a chapter every weekend. Some weekends I took a break from writing and did something else. Other weekends, I read or caught up on some editing. But I had a schedule to fall back on and that schedule helped me to finish my first book. Each writer has to find a schedule that works for her and stick to it. There are no firm rules. One writer may take a year to write a book, another may take two years, another six months. Each writer has to make the most of her situation.

Some writers face real hindrances to their writing. In order to move forward, they need to identify those hindrances and decide how best to deal with them. If you aren't writing at the level that you want to be writing, ask yourself if there's something standing in your way. Some demands on your time that keep you from writing may actually be higher-priority items, like your job or family commitments. You want to focus on hindrances that are nonessential—like watching television.

Once you've assessed your situation and know the obstacles that are standing in the way of your writing, the hard work of coming up with an action plan can begin. You may find that you have to get to bed earlier so that you can get up before your family does and do your writing. Or you may have to cut back on Saturday treks to the mall with your friends. You'll surely have to inform your family and friends of your writing goals so that they will understand the changes in your lifestyle.

As you think about finding time to write, you should also consider finding time for two related activities: pleasure reading and studying books on the craft of writing. As a writer, you should not lose your enjoyment of reading for the pleasure of reading. The by-products of pleasure reading are that you'll be up-to-date on the kinds of books published by different publishers and you'll find yourself analyzing how other writers write and learning from them.

Books on the craft of writing address the various technical aspects of writing, from plotting to creating characters to coming up with story ideas. You name it; there's a book about it. Reading books on the craft of writing is important, but you derive the greatest benefit from such books when you read them as you're writing your story. Some writers want to read all the writing books they can find *before* they start writing. When they think they've learned all there is to learn about writing, they are ready to write their story. It's not a method I endorse. You learn to write by writing, not by reading about how to write. If you're reading craft books as you write, you'll be able to apply what you're learning.

My personal bookshelf is full of writing books. The following list includes the ones I've found most helpful. Before adding any of them to your bookshelf you may want to check them out of the library or browse through them in the bookstore.

Self-Editing for Fiction Writers, Renni Browne and Dave King. I cannot say enough good things about this book. If you're almost finished with your story, this book will help you polish it.

The 20 Most Common Writing Mistakes and How to Avoid Them, Judy Delton. A very basic book with information that we all need to know.

The Weekend Novelist, Robert J. Ray. This book is a step-by-step, weekend-by-weekend guide to writing your novel in fifty-two weeks.

The Elements of Grammar, Margaret Shertzer and *The Elements of Style*, Strunk & White. There is no excuse for grammatical errors. If you're prone to them, get these two books or take a class. The small size of these volumes allows you to carry them around in your purse or pocket. You can pull them out when you have a free moment and refresh yourself on grammar basics.

Make Your Words Work, Gary Provost. I love this book. Writing is putting words on paper. Provost shows how to find the right words.

Techniques of the Selling Writer, Dwight Swain; *The Writer's Journey*, Chris Vogler; and *Screenplay: The Foundations of Screenwriting*, Syd Field. Each of these books takes you through the entire process of structuring a story. They are well worth reviewing.

Papyrus Companion: The Black Writer's Phrase Book, Ginger Whitaker & Edwina Walker. This compilation of descriptive phrases and tags is good to have, but easy to misuse. Use it to give yourself ideas about phrasing and description. Do not copy the phrases directly into your story.

The *Writer's Digest*. Elements of Fiction series: *Plot*; *Scene and Structure*; *Characters and Viewpoint*; *Theme and Strategy*; and others. This series of books by *Writer's Digest* covers the entire spectrum of writing topics.

The Career Novelist, Donald Maass. This book is a must-read for anyone interested in a career in writing. Maass is straightforward and gives information about the business of writing and publishing that every aspiring career novelist needs to know.

Writer's Digest magazine. This magazine is a good resource. The articles are straightforward and cover topics of interest to most new writers, from generating story ideas to finding a market for your work.

American Visions magazine, *Quarterly Black Review of Books* and *Black Issues Book Review*. You must subscribe to one, if not all, of these magazines. Reading them will keep you up to date on the latest news about black books and authors.

EXERCISE 3

3.1. The following questions will help you begin to identify the hindrances to your writing:

3.1.1. What should you be doing now to move forward with your writing? If you aren't doing these things, make a list of the activities and commitments that prevent you from doing them.

3.1.2. Are your family and friends aware of your need to write? Are they supportive? If they aren't, what can you do to compensate for their lack of support? If they are, how do you show them that you appreciate their support?

3.2. Answer the next two questions to give yourself some insight into steps to take to overcome your hindrances.

3.2.1. What are you willing to give up, or sacrifice, to become a better writer?

3.2.2. Do you belong to a writers support group of some kind, for example, a critique group or a readers group? Your local library or college is a good place to find such groups. If there are no such groups in your area, then you might ask your local librarian to start a list of patrons interested in forming one.

3.3. Complete the Goal-Setting Worksheet below. If the timelines presented on the worksheet don't work for you, modify them to meet your lifestyle and your needs. The key to accomplishing your goals is setting realistic ones. The only thing worse than having no goals is having goals that you have no chance of achieving.

GOAL-SETTING WORKSHEET

For writing:

I will write _____ pages each _____ .

OR

I will write for _____ hours each _____ .

I will start on _____ .

For reading craft books:

I will read _____ craft book(s) each _____ .

OR

I will read craft books for _____ hours each _____ .

My first/next craft book will be _____ .

I will start it on _____ .

For reading genre books:

I will read _____ genre book(s) each _____ .

OR

I will read genre books for _____ hours each _____ .

My first/next genre book will be _____ .

I will start it on _____ .

TWO

TELLING STORIES, WRITING BOOKS

~~~~~~

I was born in Tucker, Ark. We lived in a cabin, were sharecroppers and had a pump in the front yard. My mother had a few books, including the Bible, a Sears and Roebuck catalog, and a book with pen drawings. I used to study those drawings and try to figure out what they meant and would make up stories. That's the very beginning of my creative nature and process, I think.

—Terris Grimes (author of *Blood Will Tell*,
a Theresa Galloway mystery),
American Visions magazine, 1997

TELLING STORIES

Stories are about conflict. Conflict is about opposing forces. Man against man. Man against self. Man against nature. Without conflict there is no story. How well do you think *Waiting to Exhale* would have sold if Bernadine, Savannah, Gloria, and Robin had been content in committed relationships with men who loved them dearly? Can you imagine the movie *Soul Food* with sisters who agreed on everything? How about *Independence Day* without the threat of global destruction? Without conflict, there is no story.

Would you buy a book about a boy who rode his bike to the store to get some bread, then returned safely home? Why should you? On the other hand, you probably would want to read a book about a boy who left home on his bike headed for the store to purchase formula for his baby brother but who, four hours later, hadn't come back. This story grabs you right away. You want to know what happened to the boy.

In general, conflict is what stands between the character and her goal. What makes *Waiting to Exhale* a good story is that something stands between Savannah and the love she so desperately wanted to find. *Independence Day* is thrilling because aliens threaten to destroy civilization as Will Smith's character knows it.

This setup of character, goal, and denial-of-goal is essential to your story. Your main character has to have a goal and some opposition to accomplishing the goal. This opposition is your source of conflict. Your readers keep reading because they want to know how the conflict will play out; they want to know if the characters will prevail or surrender to forces greater than themselves. Readers enjoy battling along with characters. The saying "We appreciate more that which we fight hardest to achieve" applies to the characters in your book. The harder the characters have to fight to accomplish their goals, the more the reader identifies with the characters and wants to see them prevail.

Though you can't have a story without conflict, the mere presence of any conflict does not make a story. Take the conflict of a woman who can't get to work because she can't start her car. It's a valid conflict because the woman has a goal that she can't achieve immediately. But is her conflict substantial enough to build a story around? No. Not on the surface, anyway, because the stakes are not high enough. The woman could easily call a cab and get to work. Or she could catch the bus. Or ask one of her friends to take her. A conflict that is easily resolved is not a substantial conflict.

So, in order to create stories, we don't just need a conflict, we need a substantial conflict, or a conflict that is not easily resolved. Do you think you could write a novel about a woman who leaves her husband because of something she erroneously thought she overheard him say to one of his female employees? You could, but you wouldn't have a very strong story. Why? Because the conflict can be resolved easily. All the woman has to do is ask her husband what he said to the woman and the conflict is resolved. Conflicts that sustain books cannot be based on misunderstandings that could easily be resolved with a short conversation. The conflict has to be more substantial.

Let's go back to the woman who was eavesdropping on her husband. How can we improve this conflict? First, we can add some history to the situation. Suppose the employee is someone the husband once had an affair with. By introducing this history, we've raised the stakes. The wife is no longer reacting to an isolated conversation, but to her husband's history of infidelity.

You could also raise the level of conflict by changing the misheard conversation into a clearly understood conversation in which the husband, whose wife stopped sleeping with him a year ago after she miscarried their second child, flirts with a female employee with whom he previously had an affair. Now we have set up a genuine conflict. The wife has caught the husband doing wrong (consorting with a former lover) but she's also in the wrong (denying her husband access to her bed). Given this setup, it's unclear what the "right" course of action is for either of them. Add to the mix that the husband desperately loves his wife and your conflict grows even greater. This is genuine conflict because there are no clear-cut right answers.

Conflict is the foundation of story. Plots are built around conflict and conflict drives your plot. Characters are created with conflict in mind and conflict makes characters interesting. Every lead character in your story (hero, heroine, villain) must have a conflict that is sustainable for the length of your book. Without it, your book will fall flat.

Fictional characters are often driven by either external conflict and/or internal conflict. External conflict is conflict that originates and exists outside the character: man against nature—someone fighting to save his family from a coming tornado; or man against man—a sheriff trying to protect his town from an escaped mass murderer. With external conflict, the character has a goal that is being challenged by an external force like a tornado or a mass murderer on the loose. Mysteries, suspense stories, thrillers, and adventure stories usually have external conflicts at the center of the story. These stories are often called plot-driven stories.

Internal conflict is conflict that originates and exists within the character. Internal conflict arises out of who the character is. For example, a woman who can't commit in a new relationship because of scars she carries from a previous relationship or a man who no longer believes in himself because he no longer believes in God are both struggling with internal conflicts. An internal conflict often describes a character's struggles with himself and his beliefs. Relationship books, romances, and family sagas usually have internal conflicts at the center of the story. These stories are often called character-driven stories. Character growth, a must for all stories, is shown through internal conflict in both character-driven and plot-driven books.

Creating conflict comes easily to some writers. Unfortunately, I'm not one of them. Recently I was asked to contribute a short story for an anthology. The short story had to be a romance with a vacation theme and it had to be set outside the continental United States. Given those parameters, my first task was to come up with a question around which I could build the story. After thinking about the story for a couple of days, I came up with the question: Can a widower find love and happiness with the woman who killed his wife?

Can you see the conflict inherent in this question? What will stand in the way of the man and the woman finding happiness? Will it be the woman's guilt about her role in the first wife's death? Or will it be the man's anger at the woman for killing his wife? I chose to make it both. The conflict for the woman is overcoming her feelings of guilt; the conflict for the widower is overcoming his feelings of anger.

Would you characterize these conflicts as internal or external? If you chose internal, you're right. Both characters are struggling with internal forces (emotions) that would keep them from finding love together. Since my task was to write a short story, I chose time as the external conflict. The characters are thrown together for just one week. This short time period works against them finding love because their issues (internal conflicts) don't seem resolvable in such a short time period.

Given what you know about my story, would you characterize it as a character-driven story or a plot-driven story? If you chose character-driven, you're correct. The internal conflict drives the story and the external conflict supports the internal conflict.

There's no shame in starting your stories with simple conflicts. At this stage in writing your book, it's good not to second-guess yourself too much. Your conflict, like mine, won't be perfectly defined and it may lack the depth to sustain a book-length story, but it's a starting point. You can develop your conflict further as we discuss plotting and creating characters in the next two chapters.

EXERCISE 4

Answer the first two questions below for the books you listed in exercise 2.2.1.

4.1. Is each book plot-driven or character-driven?

4.2. What are each book's external and internal conflicts?

4.3. Is the book you're writing (or starting to write) character-driven or plot-driven?

4.4. What is the external conflict in your story?

4.5. What are the internal conflicts of each of the lead characters in your story?

WRITING BOOKS

There is some terminology we need to agree on before we move further in our discussion of the writing process. What comes to your mind when you think about the structure of a book? If you're like most people, chapters and scenes come to mind because they're the observable breaks in a book. Chapters are easily identified, scenes are a bit more difficult.

Scenes tend to cause writers trouble because the word has more than one meaning. The first kind of scene is a subunit of a chapter. From this point forward, we will refer to this type of scene as a *book scene*. Book scenes are separated within a chapter by blank lines, called scene breaks. If you don't know what I'm talking about, pick up a book that you've read. Go to chapter 1 and skim through the first few pages. Stop when you come to a blank line. Everything before that blank line is one book scene. Everything between that blank line and the next blank line is another book scene.

The second kind of scene is a unit of action taking place over a finite period of time in a specific setting. This type of scene we will refer to as a *story scene*. The story scene is best understood when looked at from a movie perspective. When talking to a friend about a movie you've both seen, I'm sure you've started more than one thought with, "Do you remember that scene where [when] . . ." With your question you are referring to a specific sequence or unit of action in the movie. Suppose I asked: Do you remember that scene in *The Nutty Professor* when the Eddie Murphy and Jada Pinkett characters are in the comedy club? If you've seen the Eddie Murphy version of *The Nutty Professor*, you'll probably ask which comedy club scene. If I clarify the scene as the comedy club scene where the comedian embarrasses Eddie Murphy's character, I'm sure you'll have no problem bringing it to mind.

For the new writer confusion arises because the book scene and the story scene don't have to be the same and many times aren't. The story scene may comprise a single book scene or it may span multiple book scenes. We will cover the details of the story scene and the book scene in chapter 8, but for now just know that as we discuss plotting and characters in the next two chapters, our focus will be on story scenes.

EXERCISE 5

Answer the following questions for each book you listed in exercise 2.2.1.

5.1. How many book scenes are in the first three chapters of each book?

5.2. Can you identify the first story scene? Don't be alarmed if you can't; you'll learn more about them in a later chapter.

THREE

THE PLOT THICKENS

~~~~~~

Plotting is the breath of a fiction story. Without it all you have is a lifeless shell. If there is no plot, there is no story to remember.

—Evelyn Coleman
(author of *What a Woman's Gotta Do*)

PLOTTING

Which comes first, the plot or the characters? There is no right answer to this question. The choice belongs to the writer. Some writers start with characters with well-defined internal conflicts and build the plot around them. Other writers start with plot. They come up with a sustainable conflict, weave a plot around it, and then they create characters that fit the story. Though the descriptions of the two methods make them seem distinct and separate, in actuality the process of building plot and creating characters is an integrated one.

Writers who use the plot-first method don't usually start with a fully fleshed out plot, rather they start with a story idea. Suppose the writer wants to write a story about a woman who hunts down the man who killed her father. That brief sentence is not the plot of the book; it's a story idea, or plot idea. From this story idea, the writer develops a story question, as we did in the previous chapter. This idea could be posed as the question, Can a nonviolent woman track down the man who murdered her father and kill him in cold blood?

From this question, the external and internal conflicts for the characters can be developed.

The process of identifying the internal and external conflicts begins with questions. Why was her father killed? Why does she feel the need for vengeance? Suppose the father was killed because he was getting ready to testify in a major criminal case. The daughter, a district attorney, feels the need for vengeance because she persuaded him to testify in spite of her concerns for his safety. The internal conflict for the daughter is whether she will allow her father's murder and her guilt to destroy her belief in right and wrong and her faith in the criminal justice system. The external conflict is whether the criminals who killed her father will kill her before she can kill them.

At this point, the writer has a story idea and starting definitions of internal and external conflicts for her characters, but he still does not have a fully developed plot. To build the plot, the writer continues to ask questions about his story. For example, how will the woman track down the villain? How will the villains track down the woman? In answering these questions, the writer builds his plot and, in the process, makes some major decisions about his characters.

One major decision we have made is that the daughter is a district attorney. Writers create their characters, so the choice of her job is not an accident. We might have chosen to make her a short-order cook, or a teacher, or a business executive. But by making her a district attorney, we heighten the conflict. Not only is the story about a daughter avenging her father's death, but it's about a district attorney turning her back on the law to avenge a personal wrong.

Writers who use the character-first method work in much the same way. Suppose the writer wants to write a story about a female family court judge who was physically abused as a child. All sorts of plot ideas open up from this brief description. Is the story about the woman reliving her past as she listens to the horror stories of the people who come before her? Or is it about a mentally deranged father stalking her after she rules against him? The writer has countless options from which to choose. Suppose the writer gives this female judge a husband and three teenaged children. The addition of family opens up more plot possibilities. Now the writer can pursue a story about a family court judge whose husband is abusive to her and their children. As you can see, the more precisely you define your characters, the better you define the plot possibilities for your story.

Though the plot-first and character-first methods usually play themselves out in an integrated manner, I will present each in a separate chapter. Since my personal preference is to start with a plot idea, we'll look at plotting first.

What Is Plot?

Sometimes people use the terms *plot idea* and *plot* interchangeably, but they have different meanings. A plot idea is an encapsulation of the story into a one- or two-sentence summary. A few pages ago we hatched a plot idea for a story about a woman who hunts down the man who killed her father. That brief statement is not a plot because it doesn't tell us how the story unfolds. Plot, as used in this discussion, tells how the story unfolds; it is the series of significant events, or story scenes (remember this term from chapter 3), that make up your story.

Think about a book you've read recently. Can you state the plot idea? You probably can. The book may have been about a wife who wakes up from a coma to find her husband in love with her best friend. Or it may have been about a black domestic in an upper-class white family who discovers the dead body of the family patriarch and is forced to track down the killer. For most stories, the plot idea is pretty easy to state.

Now think about that same book again. Can you state the

plot succinctly? This is usually where people run into problems. Some people will give only the brief plot idea when asked to give the plot of a story, while others will start at the beginning and tell you everything that happens in the story. The former is not enough information and the latter is too much. Other people fall into a third category. These people have trouble deciding what they should include and what they should leave out in their telling of the plot. These people usually spend a lot of time saying, "Hmm, let me see, it was about . . ."

The person who gives too little information, the person who gives too much information, and the person who can't decide which information to give are all suffering from the same problem: they are unable to distill the story into a series of key events, or story scenes.

Writers have similar problems when creating the plot for a story. Some writers say they don't like to plot a book before they write it because plotting takes away the fun of discovery during the writing process. I refer to these people as natural storytellers. They have an innate ability to pace the action of their story and to keep track of all the events that occur without the support that plotting provides. If you're one of these people, I salute you and encourage you to do what works best for you. Since I'm not in that elite group, I would be terrified to start a book without a plot outline.

I like to refer to the plot that I develop before I write my story as a *plot outline*, because the word *outline* reminds me that what I have developed is a guide. A guide is something I follow as needed. If I choose to divert from the guide, I merely update it to reflect my change in course so that I'll always have some sense of where I am. The guide, or in this case the plot outline, is a safety net. If I get lost in the telling of my story, the plot outline brings me back to a familiar place.

Some writers would find the level of detail in my plot outline too shallow. Theirs are so detailed that few additional decisions have to be made as they're writing their story. Some writers take a page or two to describe each story scene in the book. I find this level of detail a bit too confining. Such a detailed plot outline would indeed take the adventure out of writing the story. But that's my preference. If a detailed plot outline works for you, then you should develop one. Intricate mysteries and suspense stories may require such detail. Let your preference and the needs of your story direct you. In his book, *Writing the Blockbuster Novel*, literary agent Al Zuckerman describes the process, step-by-step, that he and Ken Follett used to develop a detailed plot outline for one of Follett's bestsellers. I recommend you take a look at this book if you prefer detailed outlines.

My plot outlines tend to look much like the outlines I created back in grade school. I use a Roman numeral heading for each chapter and within each chapter I use an alphabetic heading for each book scene. My chapter and scene descriptions are brief, usually a phrase or a short sentence. Even if your goal is to generate a detailed outline, most likely you'll start with a sparse outline like the one I use and add to it as you build the details of your story.

Types of Plots

There are three types of plots: main plots, subplots, and parallel plots. The *main plot* is the primary focus of the story. The main plot usually comes to mind when someone asks you what a book is about. In an adventure story, the main plot is the adventurer's journey. In the mystery, it's the sleuth's uncovering of clues to discover the killer. In the romance, it's the growing relationship between the hero and heroine.

A *subplot* is a secondary problem in the story that involves a main or supporting character. In an adventure story, the subplot could be the protagonist's relationship with his guide;

in a mystery, perhaps the sleuth's relationship with his mother; in a romance, it could be the hero and heroine's battle for control of the company they jointly run.

The *parallel plot* runs alongside the main plot and doesn't involve the two main characters. Unlike the subplot which is always secondary to the main plot, the parallel plot may be equally significant to the main plot in some stories. An example will help clarify the differences between the subplot and the parallel plot.

Terry McMillan's *Waiting to Exhale* is a story with a main plot (Savannah's story) and subplots (the stories of Robin, Bernadine, and Gloria). If the stories of the other women had been given the same weight as Savannah's story, then the plots would have been considered parallel plots.

Katherine Stone makes effective use of parallel plots. Most of her stories have a main plot that revolves around the relationship between two of the major characters, and one or more parallel plots that center on the relationships of other couples in the story. Each couple has an independent story but all the story lines intersect and have a similar theme.

Subplots and parallel plots, which I'll collectively refer to as *supporting plots* from this point forward, add depth and breadth to your story. They provide mechanisms for you to explore multiple dimensions of your characters and their conflicts. The plot outline helps you to keep track of your plots. When planning your story, you should construct a plot outline for the main plot and the supporting plots. Your supporting plots and your main plot should be interwoven so as to present a unified story to the reader.

Soap operas illustrate how main plots and supporting plots intersect and amplify one another. Most soap operas have four or five ongoing stories at any point in time. For example, on the CBS soap *The Young and the Restless*, Neil, Dru, Olivia, and Malcolm are usually involved in a story with a main plot that includes the four of them and supporting plots that include other characters on the show. The baby story line, in which Neil wanted to have a baby and thought Dru did too, is analogous to a novel's main plot. Olivia's secret love for Neil and how that affects her counsel to Neil and Dru is analogous to a novel's supporting plot.

There are differences between how you'll plot your book and what the soap writers do for television. First, soap opera story lines are notorious for carrying on a long time, sometimes years! Your story has to be told in a reasonable number of pages, usually no more than 500 manuscript pages and often fewer. Second, soap writers can write story lines that are independent of other story lines. In your book, the story lines should be related and, in most cases, interwoven. Third, soaps have a reputation for leaving loose ends and for changing characters' histories to accommodate the comings and goings of their actors. In a book, you must wrap up all your story lines, leaving no loose ends, and you must write your characters with consistency. If your protagonist is an orphaned only child when the story starts, parents and siblings can't pop up in chapter 10 without an explanation.

BUILDING THE PLOT OUTLINE

To build a plot outline you need story scenes and you need to know where to place those story scenes in your book. In the following sections, I'll present a plot structure technique to help you decide the most effective placement of your story scenes and a few plot development tools and techniques to help you identify your story scenes.

PLOT STRUCTURE

Plot structure is the frame for your story. Your story will ebb and flow according to the structure that you build. While different types of stories have different elements, all stories have a common goal: to keep the reader riveted to the pages. As a writer you accomplish this goal by effectively pacing the action of your story. Plot structure will help you achieve this pacing. I refer to the simple technique that I use to structure my stories as Plotting by Genre. Before we get into the details of the technique, we first need to define four key terms: genre, set piece, plot point, and character growth.

Definitions

Genre refers to the classification scheme that publishers use for books. Mystery, romance, science fiction, thriller, western, adventure, and fantasy are all fiction genres. Usually the labels can be found on the spine of the book. Books without a genre designation are referred to as mainstream fiction, or fiction that transcends genre. Publishers designate a book as mainstream or genre based on the book's target market.

Publishers of genre fiction tend to provide guidelines that specify the characteristics of the stories they publish. The guidelines can be as detailed as specifying the word count of the manuscript, the ages of the main characters, the level of sensuality or grisly detail, and acceptable settings. Or they can be as brief as "We want a compelling story." Publishers of mainstream fiction usually don't provide guidelines. If they are provided, they're of the "compelling story" variety.

Plot point, a term Syd Field uses in his book *The Foundations of Screenwriting*, denotes a movement in the story where a major incident or event occurs that spins the story in a new or unexpected direction. Plot points are opportunities for the writer to raise the stakes for the characters—and the readers. Placed strategically within the story, plot points keep the story moving at an effective pace.

Set piece, a term Ansen Dibell uses in his book *Plot*, refers to a key story scene. Set pieces are those key story scenes that drive your book, that have major implications for your characters and your story. All the other story scenes in your book lead to or result from a set piece. Two set pieces are common to all books: the opening story scene and the ending story scene.

Character growth is the change in and development of your main characters from the opening set piece to the ending set piece. In *Writer's Journey*, Chris Vogler refers to the action and events occurring between the opening and the ending as the "character's journey." The character changes as a result of his experiences along the way. As a result, he is not the same person when the story ends that he was when the story began. This change may be for the better, in which case it is called character growth, or it could be for the worse.

Now that we've defined our terms, we can move on to a discussion of the plotting-by-genre technique.

Plotting by Genre

The process of building a plot outline using the plotting-by-genre method has four steps.

Step 1. Decide if you're writing genre fiction or mainstream fiction.

In this step, the writer decides if her story can be categorized as one of the fiction genres. If the story cannot be categorized as one of the fiction genres, then it is considered mainstream fiction. If you're writing genre fiction and you have a specific publisher in mind, you should write to the publisher and request their guidelines.

Step 2. Determine the number and placement of plot points in the story.

The number and placement of plot points depends on the length of your book. Generally 75,000-word books (about 300 manuscript pages, using the standard formula of 25,000 words per 100 manuscript pages) can be plotted with five plot points while 100,000-word books (about 400 manuscript pages) require about six plot points. You should choose the number that works best for your story.

The number and placement of the plot points in your story should be chosen with two considerations in mind: maintaining reader interest and preventing the sagging middle. Therefore, you should always place a plot point at the beginning, middle, and end of your story. Depending on the length of your book, you should add one or more plot points between the opening and middle plot points, and one or more between the middle and ending plot points. Using this placement for your plot points lessens the likelihood of your story falling victim to the dreaded sagging middle.

A word of caution. Don't let the difference of one plot point in the short book and the long book mislead you into thinking that there is little difference in the effort required to write the books. As you'll see from the examples presented later in this chapter, there is a significant difference in complexity between a long book and a short book. This difference results in significantly more work for the writer of long books.

Step 3. Identify a set piece to associate with each plot point.

After you position your plot points and thereby know where your significant story movements should occur, you have to decide what those significant story movements are.

Placing a set piece at each plot point will make sure that a key story event occurs at each strategically placed plot point. For example, you may decide to have a dog die unexpectedly in your story. If this event will be a set piece—if it will have a dramatic impact on your characters, you'd place it at a plot point. If the dog's death doesn't have such an effect, then you'd want to place it elsewhere.

Set pieces accommodate the way most writers write their stories. Stories rarely come to writers in the order that the scenes appear in the book. Sometimes the first thing that comes to mind is the ending. Sometimes it's the moment of confrontation. Other times it's the opening. For many writers, the story comes in the form of these key scenes and they build the other scenes around them. For example, if the opening, climax, and ending scenes come to you first, you'll have to develop the scenes that lead you from that opening scene to the climax scene and those that lead you from the climax scene to the ending scene.

Step 4. Identify your remaining story scenes.

The character development concept comes into play at this step. Your goal is to create a story in which your character develops (grows and changes) in response to the events he or she experiences in the story. This doesn't mean that the character won't repeat the same mistakes, but it means that repeated mistakes take on new significance to the story as a whole, or to your characters.

For example, suppose that your lead character is a petty thief who is arrested and released early in the story. If the character is caught stealing again, and is arrested again, the second arrest shouldn't be a repeat of the first. The character or his circumstances should be affected, somehow by this second offense. Maybe he doesn't get caught, and getting off a second time makes the thief cocky enough to try his hand at a larger crime. Or maybe getting off a second time makes him reconsider his lifestyle and he gives up stealing. Or maybe he doesn't get off the second time. This decision is dictated by your story.

We'll discuss character development in more detail in the next chapter. For now, keep in mind these two points when identifying your remaining story scenes:

1. Each story scene must result from or lead to a set piece, *and*

2. Each story scene must show the character change as a result of what he or she has experienced in the story up to that point.

Those four simple steps are the plotting-by-genre method. In the following three examples, I use the method to develop the plot structure for a long mainstream story (400 pages; 100,000 words) and two short stories (300 pages; 75,000 words), one mainstream and one genre.

EXAMPLE 1
Longer Mainstream Book

Though the method is called plotting by genre, it can be used to plot long mainstream books. These books can be plotted using the following sequence of plot point–set piece combinations:

Plot point 1–set piece: The opening. The opening set piece introduces the lead characters and the story conflict and moves the story toward the next plot point. You should begin this set piece as close to the start of the book as possible, preferably on page 1.

Plot point 2–set piece: Depends on the story. This plot point represents the first major turn (or key event) in the story. This plot point should occur at the end of chapter 3, or around pages 45 to 50.

Plot point 3–set piece: Depends on the story. This plot point represents the second major turn (or key event) in the story and should be planned to occur around page 100.

Plot point 4–set piece: Depends on the story. This plot point represents the third major turn (or key event) in the story and should be planned to occur at the midpoint of the book, usually around page 200. The introduction of a plot point at the midpoint of the book provides protection against the sagging middle.

Plot point 5–set piece: Depends on the story. This plot point is the fourth major turn (or significant event) in the story and should be planned to occur around page 300. The significant event at this plot point, sometimes called the climax, should lead directly to the resolution.

Plot point 6–set piece: The resolution. The story conflict is resolved here. Plan to start the resolution around pages 375 to 380.

These six plot points define the structure of the long mainstream book, and serve as the frame for its plot outline. As you can see, it provides no details about what actually happens in the story.

If your story were a mystery, you could have provided set pieces that were more descriptive of the action that occurs at the plot points. For example:

Plot point 1–set piece: The murder.

Plot point 2–set piece: Discovery of the murder.

Plot point 3—set piece: Red herring.

Plot point 4—set piece: Red herring.

Plot point 5—set piece: Final clue.

Plot point 6—set piece: The case is solved.

Depending on the length of the mystery and the intricacy of the plot, more plot point–set piece combinations can be added to represent additional significant clues and more red herrings. This example is about right for a 400-page book.

EXAMPLE 2
Shorter Mainstream Book

If the story is a shorter mystery of around 75,000 words (300 manuscript pages), you should consider limiting yourself to five plot points. To accomplish this, you could eliminate the murder set piece and open your story with the discovery of the murder. For example:

Plot point 1—set piece: Discovery of the murder.

Plot point 2—set piece: Red herring.

Plot point 3—set piece: Red herring.

Plot point 4—set piece: Final clue.

Plot point 5—set piece: The case is solved.

Alternatively, you could combine plot points 4 and 5. For example:

Plot point 1—set piece: The murder.

Plot point 2—set piece: Discovery of the murder.

Plot point 3–set piece: Red herring.

Plot point 4–set piece: Red herring.

Plot point 5–set piece: Final clue solves the case.

Your story will determine whether you choose the first sequence or the second.

EXAMPLE 3
Short Inspirational Romance with Publisher Guidelines

Publishers of the shorter (around 300 pages) genre novels usually provide writers' guidelines. Having a copy of those guidelines in hand when developing your plot structure can be helpful. The following example shows the detail you can add to your plot structure when you have guidelines in hand.

The short inspirational romance has the following five plot point–set piece combinations:

Plot point 1–set piece: The meet. The guidelines specify that the hero and heroine should meet early in the story, preferably on page 1.

Plot point 2–set piece: Emotional intimacy. The guidelines specify that the relationship between the hero and heroine should be based on emotional intimacy related to their faith. This plot point and set piece reflect the attainment of the emotional intimacy level in the relationship between the hero and heroine. In a secular romance, this phase could include physical intimacy as well, but physical intimacy is not permitted in inspirational romances.

Plot point 3–set piece: Emotional commitment. As defined in the guidelines, emotional commitment is the next level of the developing relationship.

Plot point 4–set piece: Crisis. The guidelines specify that the hero and heroine must experience a crisis related to their individual faith challenges before they can have a life together.

Plot point 5–set piece: The resolution. According to the guidelines, the hero and heroine must resolve their faith challenges independently (i.e., get right with God) and come together in renewed commitment.

Of course, publisher guidelines don't include the terms *plot point* and *set piece.* Your goal when reading the guidelines should be to distill the information provided into set pieces and set points. The more detailed the guidelines, the easier this task will be.

EXERCISE 6

6.1. If you're writing a genre story and you have a publisher that you're targeting, write to that publisher and request guidelines.

6.2. Using the first three steps of the plotting-by-genre method, identify the plot points in your story and develop a two- to three-word general description for each of the associated set pieces. It's likely that you won't be able to identify a set piece for each plot point on your first try. Don't worry about it. We'll work more on identifying set pieces in the next section of this chapter.

PLOT DEVELOPMENT TOOLS

Now that you have some idea where to place the set pieces in your story, let's move on to the tools for identifying the set pieces and building the plot outline. I recommend a two-step process of free-writing and outlining. Both tools support idea generation and story development. They won't yield a fully developed plot outline, but they will give you a good start on one. We'll continue development of the plot outline in our discussion of characters in the next chapter.

Free-writing

Free-writing is a tool that writers often use when starting a book. In free-writing, you write down everything you know about the story and the characters. If you have dialogue, you include it. If you have description, you include it. If you don't know something, you make note of it. The output of the free-writing exercise is a draft story description.

There are only three rules for free-writing:

1. Write the story that's in your head.

2. All ideas are good.

3. Don't edit yourself. You're trying to get the ideas out of your head and onto the paper. You can edit later.

Outlining

Outlining most often happens after the free-writing exercise. The story description from the free-writing exercise and the plot point–set piece combinations from the plot structure are used as input to the outline. Rarely is every detail of the story description used in the outline, and invariably the story changes and firms up during the outlining process.

The outline should be viewed as a tool to help you write your story. You shouldn't force yourself to stick to it religiously. If the story dictates changes as you're writing, you should go with those changes and update the outline to reflect them. The outline serves as a crutch for you to fall back on if you get stuck in the writing of your story. With the outline, you always have somewhere to go.

The following two examples show how free-writing and outlining are used to develop the plot outline. The first example describes the process for a short genre story, and the second, for a longer mainstream story.

EXAMPLE 4
Free-writing and Outlining (Short Genre)

This example represents a free-writing and outlining exercise that I did for *The Gift of Love*, a 25,000-word inspirational novella that was to be included in an anthology of vacation stories set in locations outside the United States. The story question was: Can a man find happiness with the woman responsible for his wife's death?

Contrary to the rule of free-writing, I confess to minor editing of the story description in order to make the passage usable for teaching purposes. Because grammar and structure are not important when free-writing, rarely will a free-writing exercise result in a story description that is without grammatical errors and structural problems.

Free-writing (*The Gift of Love*)

Backstory

Mary Rogers was a wonderful wife to her husband, James, a wonderful mom to twins Kelley and Keelyn, and a wonderful friend to Jackie. Her death two years ago changed all their lives. Jackie blames herself because she was driving the car and because Mary had taken off her seat belt to get something for Jackie from the backseat when the accident occurred. Jackie was saved because she was buckled in; Mary died because she wasn't. Jackie was hospitalized for a month after the accident and never told anyone why Mary hadn't been buckled in.

For a time after his wife's death, James was angry with her for being so careless. He'd cautioned her more than once about riding in a car without her seat belt and he sees the accident as a result of her carelessness. By the time Jackie is released from the hospital, James has forgiven his dead wife though he still grieves for her.

James and Jackie had never been close and James had often wondered what his wife had in common with the sometimes flighty Jackie. Their shared grief over his wife brings them together and they become friends.

Jackie finds peace with James and the children but she feels guilty for her role in Mary's death. She knows she should tell James what happened but she can't bear for him to hate her and to turn her out of their lives. She loves the children as if they were hers. Soon she finds herself falling for James as well.

She feels guilty about her feelings for him—as if she killed her best friend and then tried to step into her life. As a result, she withdraws from the family. Unbeknownst to her, James is having feelings for her and the same associated guilt. So neither is surprised when a year after Mary's death, Jackie takes a job on a cruise ship, which keeps her away from home for much of the next year.

During their time apart, James accepts his feelings for Jackie as real and after much prayer decides to take a cruise on her ship so that he can spend some time with her.

Beginning of Story

Jackie has mixed emotions when she sees James. She had already realized that her feelings for him were real but she'd convinced herself that, with prayer and a full life, she could live without love. The guilt from Mary's death is still with her and she knows that secret alone keeps her and James from ever having a future together.

But when James visits her on the ship, Jackie decides to enjoy the four days they have together. On their second day together, James tells Jackie that he's there because he loves her and believes God wants them together. Jackie is shattered at his words because what she wants more than anything is so close and yet so far. Not having the courage to tell James her secret, Jackie pulls away from him.

James doesn't understand the change in Jackie and tries to make her tell him. During a heated exchange, Jackie blurts out the truth and James is taken for a loop. Talking aloud to himself, he says his first thought had been that the accident had somehow been a result of Jackie's carelessness but when he learned about the seat belts he'd known he was wrong.

Jackie is crushed by what she hears and accepts that whatever James felt for her is gone. He asks her why she didn't tell him and she tells him that she didn't want him to hate her. James sadly tells her that keeping the secret did more damage to his feelings for her than the truth ever could have.

James and Jackie spend the next day of the cruise alone with their thoughts. James finally puts his wife's death to rest and accepts that what he's learned hasn't changed his feelings for Jackie. He knows that she didn't kill his wife, that her death was according to the Lord's timing, but he wonders if he'll ever be able to make Jackie see that.

Later, James finds Jackie standing at the rail crying and he comforts her. She breaks down in his arms and tells him how Mary was the first real friend she'd ever had and how she'd never get over what she did to her. James tries to share with Jackie that Mary had gone home to be with the Lord and that she was probably looking down on them now. He then tells her that she needs to forgive herself because God's forgiven her and so has he.

Jackie then tells James how guilty she feels for loving him and for him loving her and how it seems that she's profiting from Mary's death—a death she caused. James then tells Jackie about a conversation he and Mary once had about Jackie in which Mary had said that she thought the reason the two of them didn't get along was because they were so much alike. She had even teased him that he probably would have married Jackie or some woman like her if Mary hadn't snatched him up first. James tells Jackie how that memory had slipped his mind until the night before he decided to take the cruise. He tells her that he believes the memory is a sign from God and Mary that loving Jackie was right for him.

Jackie's heart is set free at James's words and she allows the love for him that God has placed in her heart to take its rightful place.

Discussion

Though the story description does not give many details about what happens in the story, it does provide information that can help me start building my plot outline. Note these key points:

1. The main characters have a shared history, which I presented under the heading "Backstory." Backstory refers to events that happened before the start of the story. This backstory is key to the development of this story. If the couple were to meet for the first time when the novella opens, I would have a limited number of pages and a limited amount of time in which to develop their relationship. Such quick development of a relationship could cause the readers to question its stability. By giving

the couple a shared history, I give them a foundation on which to build their relationship and the story.

2. The novel covers a period of one week. I chose this time period because of the short length of the novella. Covering a longer period of time in such a short story would result in my having to "tell" the reader much of what happens. With the short interval, I can "show" the reader the story.

3. Notice also that I've defined a couple of set pieces: the meet on the ship when the story starts, the crisis when Jackie tells James her role in Mary's death, and the resolution when the couple reunite. Recall the plot structure we developed in the previous section for the short inspirational romance:

> Plot point 1–set piece: *The meet on the ship*.
> Plot point 2–set piece: Emotional intimacy.
> Plot point 3–set piece: Emotional commitment.
> Plot point 4–set piece: *Crisis—Jackie's confession*.
> Plot point 5–set piece: The resolution—reunion.

Outlining (*The Gift of Love*)

The plot outline is modeled on the plot structure as defined for the short inspirational romance. Since the word-count for the novella is 25,000 words (or approximately 100 pages), I chose to outline a six-chapter book with three scenes and about fifteen to twenty pages per chapter. This outline below represents my first attempt at plotting this novella.

Note: The Roman numeral headings denote chapters, and the alphabetic subheadings denote book scenes within the chapter.

I. Day 1

    A. James and Jackie meet on the ship [*the meet, plot point 1*]

    B.

    C.

II. Day 2

    A.

    B.

    C. [*emotional intimacy, plot point 2*]

III. Day 3

    A.

    B.

    C.

IV. Day 4

    A. James's profession of love [*emotional commitment, plot point 3*]

    B.

    C.

V. Day 5

    A.

    B. Jackie's confession and James's anger [*the crisis, plot point 4*]

    C.

VI. Days 6 and 7

    A. Jackie alone

    B. James alone

    C. Day 7—Jackie and James reunite forever [*the resolution, plot point 5*]

Discussion

The first step that I took in building the plot outline was to situate the plot point–set piece combinations within the chapters. Situating plot point 1 at the start of chapter 1 was easy since my goal in this short book was to get the hero and heroine together early. Situating plot point 5 at the end of chapter 6 was also easy. The others were not as easy to situate.

When I went back to the story description to identify specific story events for the set pieces at those plot points, I found a major problem in the story: Jackie's confession and James's anger, the crisis event of the story, was occurring on day two of the cruise. Given that this was to be a six-chapter novella covering a period of seven days, I was in deep trouble if I was going to get to the crisis on day two. To resolve this problem, I first associated a day with each chapter and then situated the remaining plots in the story in such a way that a reasonable amount of story time and page count separated them.

For example, I placed plot point 4 in the middle of chapter 5 because I didn't want the crisis to separate my couple for too many book pages. Given this placement, the couple is estranged from day five to day seven, but in terms of book pages, the estrangement only lasts a chapter.

Likewise, I placed plot point 2 at the end of chapter 2, and plot point 3 at the beginning of chapter 4. My rationale was that I needed the time and book space between the two to develop the romantic relationship from the emotional intimacy stage to the emotional commitment stage.

The placement of the plot point–set piece combinations within the chapters gives me the beginning of a plot outline. I don't yet know the details of my story, but I do know the general flow of the action. I know that from the couple's meeting on the cruise ship in chapter 1 until the end of chapter 2, my goal will be to show their relationship developing to the emotional intimacy phase. From the end of chapter 2 to the beginning of chapter 4, my goal will be to show their relationship developing from the emotional intimacy level to the emotional commitment level where James confesses his love for Jackie. From the beginning of chapter 4 to the middle of chapter 5, my goal will be to show the couple moving from emotional commitment to the crisis that will seemingly separate them forever—Jackie's confession of her role in Mary's death and James's resulting anger. And I know that from the middle of chapter 5 to the end of chapter 6, my goal will be to show the couple resolve the faith issues associated with the crisis and lead them to a reunion.

Some writers would feel comfortable starting to write their story with the information I have now. Since I'm not one of those writers, I need to develop my plot outline more fully before I can start writing. A deeper look at my characters should provide some help. We'll delve into the characters in the next chapter.

EXAMPLE 5
Free-writing and Outlining (Long Mainstream)

This example represents the initial free-writing and outlining exercise that I did for *To Kill For*, a 100,000-word mainstream suspense story. The story question for this story was similar to the one used in the previous example: Can a man find happiness with the woman who killed his wife?

Free-writing (*To Kill For*)

Backstory

Jackie and Mary had been friends since elementary school. Mary was raised in a single-parent family with a hard-working but defeated mother. Jackie, on the other hand, was the only child of parents who doted on her. Though both girls were attractive, the difference in their social status made it surprising that they were friends. Mary and Jackie considered themselves best friends until seventh grade, when James Rogers moved to town. Jackie, used to getting what she wanted, thought James should be hers as well. But James, raised in a poor, single-parent family himself, found a soulmate in Mary. The two became sweethearts in junior high and nobody was surprised when the two of them went to college in Atlanta— James to Morehouse and Mary to Spelman, both on scholarship. Of course, Jackie went to Spelman also. She would have gone just to be near James even if it hadn't been a tradition for the women in her family to attend the college.

During their college days, Jackie's jealousy of Mary and James's relationship became obvious to James. He tried to tell Mary but she wouldn't believe that about her friend, attributing it to the tension that had always existed between the man she loved and her best friend. Jackie came on to James one night. He turned her down, and fortunately Mary never found out. Jackie started dating some other guy at Morehouse, giving the appearance that she'd gotten over James.

James and Mary announced their plans to get married immediately after graduation. Jackie and her guy, Roy, immediately follow with their own wedding plans. Jackie later apologizes to James for her past behavior and tells him that now that she's found the love of her life she can be happy for him and Mary. James reluctantly accepts her apology. After their weddings, James and Mary head to Boston for graduate school, while Jackie and her husband head for Los Angeles. Distance severs the strands of their relationship and the couples don't meet again until fifteen years later. After college, Mary and James begin their careers in Atlanta.

Beginning of Story

Mary is happily surprised when she gets a call from Jackie, whom she hadn't heard from in fifteen years. She learns that Jackie's in town with her husband, who's interviewing for a job. Jackie and Mary catch up with each other. Jackie learns that Mary and James have two twin daughters, Kelley and Keelyn. Jackie and Roy don't have any children and Jackie hints that there might be problems in her relationship with her husband. Feeling compassion for her friend, Mary invites them to come over while they're in town.

James is uneasy about the visit since he still doesn't trust Jackie, but he goes along with his wife's plans. The dinner turns out to be a success. The twins are immediately taken with Jackie, who brings them gifts. And James and Roy get along like a house on fire. By the time the evening is over, both couples are excited about the possibility of Jackie and Roy moving back to Atlanta.

Roy gets the job and he and Jackie move to Atlanta and begin a close friendship with James and Mary. A short time after the move, Mary is killed in a tragic car accident. The police suspect foul play but find nothing. Jackie and Roy support James and the twins through their grief. Jackie begins to devote herself to the twins. James, blind with grief, is glad for the relief and fails to notice what's happening to Jackie and Roy's relationship. When Jackie tells him that Roy has left her, he's surprised but still too numb with grief to process the information.

Jackie has now devoted herself full-time to James and the

girls. Taking care of them helps keep her mind off her own problems. When James is finally ready to join the living again, Jackie is right there to help him. Though James had never really felt close to Jackie, he is drawn to her as they support each other in their shared grief.

As the relationship between Jackie and James blossoms, Jackie starts receiving mail implicating her in Mary's death. She tracks down the sender and they have an argument and an altercation. The man falls to his death before Jackie can find out who put him up to the dirty job. Jackie runs away without calling the police.

Shortly afterward, Jackie gets a new packet of evidence in the mail. This time it's a photo of her with the dead man. Jackie is frantic. About this time, James finally tells her that he thinks he's falling in love with her. Jackie sees herself on the verge of having everything she ever wanted, and of having that dream destroyed by the crazed person sending the letters. In spite of all this, she accepts James's proposal and begins to prepare for a wedding.

As the day of the wedding nears, the evidence continues to come to Jackie in the mail. She tries unsuccessfully to find out who's sending it. She suspects numerous people, but they're all false leads. The day before the wedding, Roy shows up and Jackie learns that he's been sending the mail. He tells her that he knows she killed Mary, and that he loved her so much that instead of turning her in, he left her. But he says he can't allow her to make a life with Mary's husband. He'd hoped she would have walked away after he starting sending the evidence, especially after the PI was killed, but she wouldn't. He gives her a final chance to call the wedding off. Jackie urges Roy to leave and tells him that she'll meet him later that night. She begs him not to do anything.

Jackie goes to see Roy that night. He tries one last time to get her to call off the wedding. When she refuses, he turns to call the police. As he turns, Jackie shoots him. She then rushes out of the room.

The next day as Jackie is walking down the aisle, police arrive at the church and arrest her. Roy is with them.

Discussion

Though the story description does not give many details about what happens in the story, it does provide information that can help me start building my plot outline. Note these key points:

1. This story description includes a significant discussion of backstory, as did the last example.

2. Jackie is not revealed as the killer until very late in the story description and no clues are given to signal her as the killer.

3. This story is much more complicated than the story presented in the previous example because this story has a main plot and a supporting plot. The main plot is the murder plot, and the supporting plot, which starts after Mary's death, is the growing relationship between Jackie and James.

4. I can glean candidate set pieces for the story. I use the term *candidate* because there are so many options with this story. There is no *right* or *wrong* set piece for a given plot point; writing is an art, not a science. The writer must use her intuition, skill, and experience to choose set points that will most effectively pace her story. Recall the plot structure we developed in the previous section for the long mainstream book:

Plot point 1–set piece: The opening. Candidate: the phone call from Jackie telling Mary about the visit,

Mary telling James about the visit, or the dinner visit.

Plot point 2–set piece: First major story turn (around pages 45 to 50). Candidate: Mary's tragic car accident.

Plot point 3–set piece: Second major story turn (around page 100). Candidates: Jackie receives first envelope with incriminating evidence; James acknowledges that he likes having Jackie in his life.

Plot point 4–set piece: Third major story turn (around page 200). Candidates: Jackie kills the guy; James confesses his love.

Plot point 5–set piece: Fourth major story turn (around page 300). Candidates: Jackie receives the note after she's killed the PI; James wants to get married.

Plot point 6–set piece: The resolution (around pages 375 to 380). Candidates: Jackie shoots Roy; Jackie's wedding.

Note that two set pieces are defined at each plot point following Mary's death, one for the murder plot and one for the relationship plot.

Outlining (*To Kill For*)

The plot outline is modeled on the plot structure as defined for the long mainstream novel. Since the word-count for the long mainstream story is about 100,000 words (or approximately 400 manuscript pages), I chose to outline a twenty-three–chapter book with three book scenes and about fifteen to twenty pages per chapter. The following outline represents my first attempt at a plot outline for this suspense story.

*   *   *

Note: The Roman numeral headings denote chapters. Because there are so many chapters in this story, I have left out the subheadings for the book scenes.

I. *Plot point 1–set piece: The opening*. The phone call from Jackie telling Mary about the visit.

II.

III. *Plot point 2–set piece: First major story turn* (around pages 45 to 50). Mary's tragic car accident.

IV.

V.

VI. *Plot point 3–set piece: Second major story turn* (around page 100). Jackie receives first envelope with incriminating evidence; James acknowledges that he likes having Jackie in his life.

VII.

VIII.

IX.

X.

XI. James confesses his love to Jackie.

XII. *Plot point 4–set piece: Third major story turn* (around page 200). Jackie kills the PI.

XIII.

XIV.

XV.

XVI.

XVII. James wants to get married.

XVIII. *Plot point 5–set piece: Fourth major story turn* (around page 300). Jackie receives the note after she's killed the guy.

XIX.

XX.

XXI.

XXII. *Plot point 6–set piece: The resolution* (around pages 375 to 380). Jackie shoots Roy.

XXIII. Jackie's wedding and arrest.

Discussion

I begin building my plot outline by placing the plot points at the page numbers suggested by the plot structure.

A complication arises because I have a main plot and at least one supporting plot, which I have to interweave through the story. As you can see from the plot outline, I chose to pair the relationship set piece and the murder set piece at plot point 3, while plot points 4 and 5 offset the set pieces by placing a relationship set piece before each of the murder set pieces. Both plots end in chapter 23 when Jackie is arrested at the church.

The placement of the plot point–set piece combinations within the chapters gives me the beginning of a plot outline, but there is too much that I don't know. For example, at this point, James has no identity in the story except as the focus of Jackie's obsession. If he is to be the multidimensional character that a book of this length requires, he must be given a life and goals of his own. The same is true for the character of Roy. Why is he secretly sending the incriminating evidence to Jackie?

We'll look at ways to give both characters substance in the next chapter.

EXERCISE 7

7.1. Following the examples presented in this section, complete the free-writing and outlining exercises for your story. Don't worry if you can't fully populate your plot outline; we'll work more on it in the next chapter when we discuss characters.

FOUR

CREATING BELIEVABLE CHARACTERS

〜〜〜〜〜〜〜〜〜〜〜〜〜〜〜〜〜〜〜〜〜〜〜

My audience is a broader audience than the normal mystery writer's. Part of that is because I'm black; part of that is, I think, I'm an OK writer. But another part of it is that I'm dealing with issues that are important issues—black male heroes, but not black male heroes whom we like out of hand. You have someone like Mouse, somebody like Easy. Though Easy's a nice guy, he does some things wrong. You have people like Soupspoon, who, in a completely different way, is not like your everyday kind of hero. The reason you like him is because if you knew somebody like him in your family, you would love him. You see his flaws, but you accept them. And that's the whole thing I've been talking about: acceptance.

—Walter Mosley
(author of *Blue Light*),
American Visions magazine, 1995

If you're like most writers, you will find creating characters a major challenge. Though your story is fiction, the characters in your story must be as real as your next-door neighbors. The extent to which you are able to create real characters determines the degree to which your readers will be able to believe and embrace them. That's what you, as a writer, want.

You want your reader to invest in your characters and to care about what happens to them.

In the previous chapter you began developing your plot outline. In this chapter you will learn to create characters to fit that plot outline. Don't be surprised if you find the need to revise your plot as you create your characters. Don't be surprised, either, if you find yourself changing your characters to make them a better fit for your plot. Though plotting and characterization are being presented in separate chapters, remember that they are a single process.

WHERE TO START

The first step in creating characters is to focus on a single character. As with television shows and movies, you may find that your novel has lead characters, supporting characters, and extras. I find it easiest to start with the main, or leading, character(s) in the story. Then I address the supporting characters, followed by the extras.

Leading Characters

Leading characters are those characters (usually one to three) around which your story revolves. Of these lead characters, you should select one as your protagonist. The protagonist is the character that you, the writer, want the reader to care most about. Also referred to as the hero or heroine, the protagonist is the character with the main story goal; thus, this character also has the main story conflict. In the mystery, the protagonist is the sleuth who solves the crime. In the romance, it's the guy who gets the girl or the girl who gets the guy.

Consider, for example, Terry McMillan's *Disappearing Acts*, the urban relationship story that addresses contemporary social issues such as racism, emotional and physical abuse, self-hate, family, love, and friendship. The lead characters in the story are Zora and Franklin; *Disappearing Acts* is about these two people. Franklin is an intelligent, good-looking man who cares deeply for Zora but he's a prisoner of fear. Disappointment sends him to the bottle and fear keeps him from moving in new directions. Zora is an intelligent, good-looking, goal-oriented woman. She's reaching for her goals and is reasonably confident she will accomplish them. She's unwise in her relationships; she's gone through quite a few men and had more than one abortion. Neither Franklin nor Zora is perfect; their imperfection makes them and their story real.

Supporting Characters

After creating my leading characters, I then move on to my secondary, or supporting, characters. Supporting characters take on the roles of the heroine's best friend, parent, or sibling; the hero's sidekick, mentor, or boss; the villain's hit man, attorney, or confidant. They serve two very important purposes in stories. First, supporting characters can be used to reveal information about your leading characters. Suppose your protagonist is a cynical, hard-as-nails cop who strikes fear in the hearts of criminals and fellow cops alike, but who cooks dinner for his elderly mother every weekend. The cop's interaction with his mother gives the reader new insight into him.

Second, supporting characters can be used to advance the plot of your story. Suppose the cop's boss assigns him to a murder case and later removes him from the case. The plot is advanced when the cop gets the case and it probably changes direction after he's removed. The supporting character, the boss, has played a pivotal role in advancing the story.

Zora's three best girlfriends—Claudette, Portia, and Marie—

are three key supporting characters in *Disappearing Acts*. They are important to the story because through them the reader gains insight into Zora. The reader can contrast Zora's relationship with Franklin to that of Claudette and her husband and to those of Portia and the men she dates. The reader can compare Marie's quest to make a success of her God-given comedic talent to Zora's efforts to do the same with her musical talents. The author carefully crafted each of these supporting characters to reveal and make more distinct the character of Zora.

Franklin's unloving and unlovable mother, another key supporting character, is important to the story because she gives the reader insight into Franklin's poor relationship skills. She also serves as a catalyst for a major plot movement. Her mistreatment of Zora at a family dinner sets off a series of actions and reactions that result in exposing Zora's battle with epilepsy, a fact she had been hiding from Franklin. This revelation moves Zora and Franklin's relationship to a new level.

A similar analysis can be made of the other supporting characters in *Disappearing Acts*. Though some of their roles carry more importance than others, each supporting character advances plot or reveals character.

Writers have to *know* their lead characters and their supporting characters. Because the story revolves around the lead characters, the writer must know their lead characters more intimately than they know their supporting characters. Supporting characters are important only because of their interaction, directly or indirectly, with the lead characters. When creating lead characters it's most effective to focus on the *person*, but when creating supporting characters it's most effective to focus on the *role* they play in relation to the lead characters.

Extras

The third category of characters in your story is what I term extras. Extras have smaller roles and less interaction with the lead character(s) than do supporting characters. Their roles are sometimes considered "props" (the waiter, the doorman, etc). Extras can be used to reveal character and advance plot just as supporting characters do. The waiter is not just a nameless, faceless person who serves the protagonist and her date at the restaurant. We learn something about the protagonist by her interaction with the waiter. Her response, or lack of response, to the waiter reveals something about her, though we may learn little or nothing about the waiter in the same exchange. For example, you get different impressions of a heroine who remembers and uses the waiter's name and a heroine who snaps commands at him.

The nameless cabdrivers who shuttle Franklin and Zora around New York City in *Disappearing Acts* are important in revealing Franklin's character. Franklin's outrage at having to rely on Zora to hail a cab at night and his resulting hostile interaction with the cabdriver give us insight into his disenchantment with white America.

EXERCISE 8

8.1. Identify the lead characters in a book you've read recently. What makes those characters memorable? Which character is the protagonist? How do you know?

8.2. Identify the supporting characters in the same story. What do you learn about the leading characters from their interactions with the supporting characters? What role do the supporting characters play in advancing the plot?

8.3. Identify the extras in the same story. What do you learn about the leading characters from their interactions with the extras? What role do the extras play in advancing the plot?

8.4. Identify the lead characters and key supporting characters in your story.

BUT THEY ALL LOOK ALIKE

If readers are going to care about your characters, they must get to know them. They must know them by name, of course, but that's only the beginning. If you are good at creating characters, your readers will know them by their actions, their thoughts, and their mannerisms.

Think about a close friend or family member. Aren't there distinctions in this person's personality, demeanor, or appearance that allow you to say readily, "That's just like so-and-so," or "That sounds like something she would say," or "She wouldn't do anything like that." Your readers should know your characters well enough to make similar statements about them.

Think about the cast of the now-syndicated *Living Single* television series. If you described one of the *Living Single* characters as a single woman living in New York City, which character would you be talking about? It's not clear since all four women—Khadijah, Regine, Max, and Synclaire—fit that description. What if you added the details that the character is black and under thirty? Still not clear; all four women are black and under thirty. You need more details in order to identify this character. Fortunately, the series writers created full-bodied, easily distinguishable characters, which we will use as good examples of well-developed characters.

First, let's look at Khadijah. How do we distinguish Khadijah from the other three women? There's her size; she's bigger than the other three. Her language and use of slang label her as the "home girl" of the group. But Khadijah's character is deeper than that. We know that she's smart, because the sister owns and runs a magazine that she founded. We know that she's a nurturer, because the other women come to her with their problems. But being the home girl that she is, we also know that she always tells it straight and pulls no punches in her advice. Khadijah comes across as tough, but we know that underneath she's a softie.

Next is Regine. She's the shortest of the four. We know that Regine thinks she's the diva of the group because she tells us often and because she dresses the part. But what sets Regine apart are those wigs of hers and her never-ending pursuit of some rich man to take care of her. Regine is the character who has to be reminded of who she is and from whence she came. Left to herself, she'd forget.

Let's move on to Max. Max is the darkest of the four women and the only one with unpermed hair. Everything about Max screams, "I'm my own woman—a black woman—and I'm not making excuses to anybody." Max is an "I am woman, hear me roar" kind of woman. She's educated, attractive, and brassy as all get-out. She's a challenge to every man—in work and in play. Max would have us believe that she has no heart, but sometimes we catch a glimpse of one.

I saved Synclaire for last. Synclaire is the innocent of the group. She's the girl next door and as sweet as she can be, but sometimes she works your last nerve. We know Synclaire has a heart, but we sometimes wonder if she has a brain. On those occasions when she shows us that she indeed has one, we're pleasantly surprised.

We could go much further in looking at the distinctions in the characters from *Living Single*, but I think you get the idea. Khadijah, Max, Regine, and Synclaire are four single black women living in New York City, but they are distinct in appearance, personality, intellect, and insight. The characters you create must be distinct as well.

EXERCISE 9

9.1. Describe the lead characters you identified in exercise 8.1 and discuss what makes them distinct and unique characters.

9.2. Describe the supporting characters you identified in exercise 8.2 and discuss what makes them distinct and unique characters.

9.3. Describe the leading and supporting characters in your story and discuss what makes them distinct or unique. Do not be dismayed if you have trouble doing so. Before you finish this chapter, you will have the tools and techniques to make them unique.

A WORD ABOUT MOTIVATION

Motivation provides the rationale for your characters' actions and reactions. Motivation ties your characters to your plot. Characters must act or react for a reason. They must act and speak based on who they are as people. For example, it would be reasonable for an out-of-work Regine to blow off a job interview for the chance to meet a rich, single guy. It wouldn't be reasonable for an out-of-work Khadijah to do the same thing.

When Franklin (in *Disappearing Acts*) was laid off from his job for the third time, the reader was not surprised that he bought a bottle of booze and began to drink. By this point, the reader understood that drinking was how Franklin dealt with disappointment.

BUT MY CHARACTERS ARE BLACK

I want to make special note here that black writers don't have to write stories with black characters only, or stories with any black characters for that matter. You are free and encouraged to write any story that you can effectively execute. If you are black and you want to write a story that has few, if any, black characters, by all means do so. My only caveat is that your story must be authentic; it must represent reality. As minorities in American culture, blacks are in a position to provide social commentary on the system, the way things are. Minority status brings with it a mandate to understand how the majority operates if one is to succeed in the majority culture. A story written out of this perspective can be quite powerful.

TOOLS FOR CREATING CHARACTERS

Though we began developing plot outlines in the previous chapter, none of the characters we introduced were fully developed. In this section, we're going to add depth to those characters by applying some of my preferred tools and techniques: character type, the character profile, and the character interview.

You may use one or all to develop characters for your story. Using the *character interview*, you ask your characters a series of open-ended questions and allow them to answer in their own voice. Using the *character profile*, you complete a worksheet detailing over forty traits for each character. The *character type* gives you a broad description of a character which you can develop more fully using the character profile or character interview techniques.

When I wrote my first book, I started with a character type from the romance novels I'd read—the fulfilled-in-work, unfulfilled-in-love heroine—and then I used the character profile to fully describe the character. With that first book, I religiously defined every characteristic on the Character Profile Worksheet. And guess what? It helped me tremendously. Of course, I didn't use all of the information I had recorded and I even ended up changing some of it as my character came to life on the page.

By the time I started writing my third and fourth books, I had developed my own personalized way of defining characters. I start with a story idea and then move to the free-writing and outlining exercises like we did in the previous chapter. I then use the character profile and the character interview to give me a deeper understanding of my characters. I use character typing primarily to help me in selecting supporting characters and extras.

I no longer feel the need to complete every item on the Character Profile Worksheet. Instead, I complete as many as I can and then, with updated plot outline in hand, I write the first three chapters of my book. My characters seem to take on life in those chapters. Many times I don't *find* the real character until I finish the third chapter.

After finishing the first three chapters, I go back and update my character profile and my plot outline to reflect the changes and refinements I made while writing those chapters. Then I go back and rewrite the chapters to make sure that my characters are consistent throughout. Since my characters were taking shape as I was writing those first three chapters, often the characters that I started with in chapter 1 are not the same characters that I ended with in chapter 3. Sometimes personality traits change, other times relationships change. But there is always a change in the characters from the way I initially perceived them. The rewrite is necessary to ensure that the characters are consistent throughout the first three chapters before I move on.

Your method of creating characters probably will evolve as you write. Don't be alarmed; what you're experiencing is natural. You should also be careful not to become a slave to the tools. The character type, character profile, and character interview support you in your writing; use them to meet your needs and the needs of your story. In short, you control the tools; they don't control you.

GENERATING CHARACTER TYPES

A character type is a *kind*, or *category*, of character. Your hero may be a brooding bad boy or a militant genius or a conservative home boy. All three are character types. They are generalizations of the character. They don't fully describe or define the character but they give you a place to start. Character types exist in books and all around us. Two great sources of them are genre books and your immediate surroundings.

Character Types from Genre Novels

If the story you're writing is in a genre in which you've done a lot of reading, then you know the types of characters that regularly appear in those stories. These characters, called stock genre characters, can be used as character types. Consider the types of characters you're likely to find in the following genre fiction categories.

Romance. Alpha macho-man hero, beta ultrasensitive hero, the virginal heroine, the woman-about-town, the woman with a past

Mystery. The ne'er-do-well detective, the cynical ex-cop, the retired, female amateur sleuth

Suspense. The nosy neighbor, the Good Samaritan, the overly ambitious journalist

Action adventure. The hard-as-nails ex-mercenary, the money-hungry treasure hunter, the sophisticated world traveler, the staid archaeologist

Thriller. The computer whiz, the academic, the ex-CIA agent

Western. The lone ranger, the good-hearted woman of the evening, the prudish schoolmarm, the deceptively easygoing marshal

There are many more character types that you can add to each listed genre. This partial list should give you a good idea of what is meant by the term *stock genre character*.

Character Types in Your Personal Environment

Sometimes the inspiration for characters lies no farther than a bench in the local mall. Imagine the types of people you find in a mall in a predominantly black neighborhood. How do those people differ from the people you find in a mall on the other side of town? You can answer these questions and create character types at the same time.

Observations for character typing can be done formally or informally. Formal observation works best if you enjoy going to the zoo, or the mall, or the airport, or to any place that people gather. You don't have to have a story in mind when you're observing. You merely observe and record what you see. The character typing that you do today can be used in a book that you write next year.

With informal observation, you carry a notebook with you

at all times and record any observations that strike you. Jot down things you notice on the bus, in your office, in the classroom, anywhere and everywhere you go. If you don't feel comfortable carrying around a notebook, you can always make mental notes, but record them later.

The traits you could record about the people you observe are endless. The following list should give you a good start:

Physical Attributes:

Sex

Age

Height

Build

Eyes

Skin

Hair

Speaking voice

Mannerisms

Dress code

Birthmarks or scars

General health

Disabilities

Biographical Details:

Named after

Looks like

Acts like

Siblings

Birth order

Birth date

Ethnic origin

Citizenship

Marital Status

Family background

Born in

Lives in

Economic background

Current economic status

Education

Talent and skills

Occupation

Professional activities

Social activities

Hobbies

Sports

Religious preferences	Secret dreams
Political preferences	Public dreams
Emotional/Psychological Makeup:	Biggest problem
	Pet peeves
Ambition level	Likes
Moral code	Dislikes
Habits—good and bad	Biases/prejudices
Addicted to	Wants most
Fears	Strengths
Values	Weaknesses
Is impressed by	Other

The list is not meant to be definitive so feel free to add and delete traits as you deem necessary. Of course you won't have access to all this information about the people you observe. Make guesses where you can.

In addition to recording traits, you should also associate a tag with each person you observe. What comes to mind when you think of the person? It may be voice; if so you may tag the person as Mellow Lips. Or it could be the way the person uses language. In that case, you could tag the person as Miss Proper. Remember, character types aren't full descriptions of people, they're tags that bring to mind specific character traits.

Some character types are so common in our environment that we don't have to observe to find them because we already know them. For example, there are some common character types that exist across most African American communities. Consider the well-to-do funeral director, the gossipy hairdresser, the loud Baptist preacher, the activist city council member. These character types are readily recognizable and can add authenticity to your story. You can also turn the character types around for a totally different effect. How about the quiet, mousy hairdresser or the almost-invisible city council member? The possibilities are endless. These character types can be used effectively to give your story an African American *feel*.

Some people would call these character types stereotypes, and, to a certain extent, they would be correct. They are stereotypes if we define the character as the character type. But remember, character types don't define characters, they merely give you a place to start. You may begin developing your character with the gossipy hairdresser character type, but as you delve more deeply into the hairdresser, you'll find that she's a multidimensional person. The fact that she talks a lot is just a small part of the whole that makes up her personhood. Once you fully develop a character, you can no longer be accused of stereotyping.

EXERCISE 10

10.1. List some of the character types commonly found in your favorite books.

10.2. List the personality traits associated with each character type listed in 10.1.

10.3. Take an outing to a place where people gather. Create a tag for each person you observe and record your observations.

10.4. Think about the community in which you live. What roles do the people in your community play in the day-to-day workings of the community? For example, there may be teachers, ministers, newspaper delivery persons, community leaders, etc. List the traits that make each role uniquely identifiable. The next time you create a character that plays one of these roles, you may be able to use one or more of the traits you've identified here.

THE CHARACTER PROFILE

The character profile allows you to record details about your characters' traits. If you start with a character type, the character profile can help you turn that type into a fully developed character. The same is true if you start your character from a plot idea as I did in the previous chapter.

Character Profile Worksheet

As you can see on the following pages, the Character Profile Worksheet provides a basic list of character attributes. The list includes physical attributes such as height, weight, and eye color; biographical attributes such as birth date, number of siblings, and birthplace; and emotional attributes such as secret dreams, fears, and pet peeves. This list is not meant to be exhaustive or definitive; rather, it is meant to help you generate ideas for your character and your story.

When determining a character's physical appearance, I usually start with a photograph from a magazine that captures the "look" I want for the character. From there, I refine traits to make the character unique. For example, *Essence* once ran a series of ads that featured a tall, well-built, brown-skinned man in a white linen suit and matching linen cap. The man sat on the beach with a woman who was also clad all in white. The man radiated confidence and male sexuality along with a hint of boyish charm. The man so impressed me that I wrote a story that featured him as the hero. My character even wore a white linen suit in one scene. You can use this same technique when creating your characters.

A picture and a look, however, are not enough to define a character. The *Essence* man did not become a person until I gave him a background, an identity. Every character needs a psychological and social background. He has to have roots and those roots play a role in who the character is. When you begin to define these traits, you begin to make your character one-of-a-kind.

You choose traits not only to make your characters unique, but you also choose them to support the conflict and motivation of your character. For example, a gash on a man's otherwise handsome face not only serves to give him a distinctive look; it could also explain the way he treats the women in his life. Maybe he lets them walk all over him because he doesn't feel he has many options, or maybe he treats them badly because he knows that they will leave him eventually. Or maybe his personality is so charismatic that people drawn to him don't even notice it. The key point is that the scar serves as more than a physical marker on the character's face; it also represents an emotional marker on the character's psyche.

You can use the Character Profile Worksheet to help you fully develop your lead and supporting characters. The amount of detail you supply is up to you. As I mentioned earlier, you can get by with knowing less about your supporting characters than about your leading characters. On the other hand, the more you know about all of your characters, the more you have to work with when writing your story.

CHARACTER PROFILE WORKSHEET

Copy this worksheet and complete as needed for leading and secondary characters. Space is provided for you to add attributes as needed.

Name _____

Physical Attributes

Sex _____
Age _____

Height _____

Build _____

Eyes _____

Skin _____

Hair _____

Speaking voice _____
_____
_____

Mannerisms _____
_____
_____

Dress code _____
_____
_____

Birth marks and scars _____
_____
_____

General health _____
_____
_____

Disabilities _____
_____
_____

Biographical Details

Named after _____

Looks like _____

Acts like _____

Siblings _____

Birth order _____

Birth date _____

Ethnic origin _____

Citizenship _____

Marital status _____

Family background _____

_____

_____

Born in _____
Lives in _____
Economic background _____
Current economic status _____
Education _____
Talents and skills _____

_____

Occupation _____

_____

Professional activities _____

_____

_____

Social activities _____

_____

_____

Hobbies _____

_____

_____

Sports _____

_____

Religious preferences _____

_____

Political preferences _____

_____

_____

Emotional/Psychological Makeup

Ambition level _____

_____

_____

Moral code _____

_____

Habits—good and bad _____

_____

Addicted to _____

_____

Fears _____

_____

Values _____

_____

Is impressed by _____

_____

Secret dreams _____

_____

Public dreams _____

_____

Biggest problem _____

_____

Pet peeves _____

_____

Likes _____

_____

Dislikes _____

_____

Biases/prejudices _____

_____

Wants most _____

_____

Strengths _____

_____

Weaknesses _____

_____

Other _____

_____

Developing Characters Using the Character Profile

In the previous chapter, I completed the free-writing and outlining exercises and began developing the plot outline for the 100,000 word suspense novel *To Kill For*. Let's go back to that novel and further develop the outline by concentrating on the characters.

A review of the plot outline and the story description from the free-writing exercise indicates some major problems with the story as currently described:

1. Readers sometimes have difficulty keeping track of characters when their names are similar. The names of the main characters, James and Jackie, were changed to Kenneth and Jackie so that both names wouldn't start with the same letter.

2. The story description does not include a trail of Jackie's plotting and scheming from the beginning of the story through the end.

3. Though Kenneth is a major character in the story, all we know about him is that he falls in love with Jackie after his wife is killed. Kenneth needs more development. The character serves no purpose other than to prop up Jackie's story line. Kenneth needs conflict and motivation.

4. Roy, Jackie's husband, like Kenneth, needs conflict and motivation. Right now, he too, is little more than a prop to support Jackie's antics.

5. Unlike the novella, a longer book requires a broader context. At this point, it seems as though Jackie, Roy, and Kenneth live in a vacuum. They must be placed in a context where they interact with supporting characters and extras.

The last four of these concerns with the story translate into a series of questions that must be answered before the plot outline can be fully developed. We can use the character profile to answer two of those questions:

Who is Kenneth?

Who is Roy?

EXAMPLE 6
Character Profile (Roy, *To Kill For*)

Character profile traits identified for Roy:

Looks like   Kenneth

Hair   full beard

Family background   mother committed suicide in asylum

Fears   Jackie will end up like his mother

Discussion

I did not identify every trait on Roy's character profile. In fact, I left most of them blank. There was no need to record physical attributes—I have a magazine photo that I'll use for Roy's physical description. I only identified traits that I could immediately tie into the plot of the story. They were: looks like, hair, family background, and fears. I will probably need to identify more traits before the plot is fully developed and before I finish writing the story but for now I'll address these four.

The "looks like" trait has the biggest impact on my story because I chose to have Roy look like Kenneth. When I read "looks like" on the Character Profile Worksheet, the idea immediately came to me. This choice has major implications for the backstory and what happens in the story:

1. This resemblance of the two men indicates the level of Jackie's obsession with Kenneth: she couldn't have Kenneth so she married a man who looked just like him.

2. For the story to have the greatest impact, Roy shouldn't realize that he looks like Kenneth until he and Jackie arrive at Kenneth and Mary's house for dinner. I'll have to change the backstory so that Mary, Kenneth, Jackie, and Roy didn't go to college together and didn't attend each other's weddings.

3. Because of its ramifications on the characters and story, the dinner scene is clearly a set piece in the story.

4. So that Roy is the only person to realize the resemblance, I had to give Roy a full beard (trait: hair). If he were clean-shaven, Mary and Kenneth would recognize the resemblance as well.

5. The initial story description hinted at a problem in Roy and Jackie's relationship. With the resemblance angle, I can now have their problems rooted in Jackie's mental instability as evidenced by her obsession with Kenneth. Jackie's mental instability adds another angle to the story.

6. As written, the story description doesn't give a reason why Roy would love his wife so much that he would protect her from the police, even after she's left him to be with Kenneth. His family background and fears provide the reason: Roy's mother committed suicide while institutionalized and he wants to save Jackie from that fate.

7. Roy's battle to save Jackie from herself becomes a new supporting plot in the story. This subplot leads to the creation of a new supporting character, the police detective heading the investigation into Mary's death.

This example shows clearly that we advanced the plot of the story by using the Character Profile Worksheet to better understand the characters. As Roy's character is taking shape, the story is also taking shape.

Let's stop for a moment with Roy, and see what we can do about bringing Kenneth to life.

EXAMPLE 7
Character Profile (Kenneth, *To Kill For*)

Character profile traits identified for Kenneth:

Named after   his father

Looks like   Roy

Acts like   spoiled brat

Birth order   only child

Hair   clean-shaven

Dress code   stylish, spiffy

Marital status   married

Family background   stable

Born in   Atlanta suburbs

Lives in   Atlanta suburbs

Economic background   lower middle class

Economic status   upper middle class

Education   advanced degree

Occupation   accountant in his mother's church

Social life   womanizer

Religious prefs   hypocrite

Morality   none

Fears   living his father's life

Values   money

Is impressed by   things

Likes women

Dislikes his mother

Values his children

Wants most to have his cake and eat it too

Discussion

I did not identify every trait on Kenneth's character profile, but I identified significantly more traits for him than I did for Roy. There was no need to record physical attributes since I know that Kenneth looks like Roy when Roy's not sporting a beard. Instead, I chose to identify those traits that gave me insight into Kenneth's family background and how that background has influenced the man he is today. The picture of Kenneth presented by those identified traits is very different from the picture of Kenneth painted in the initial version of the story description. The character profile traits paint Kenneth as a selfish and materialistic womanizer who dislikes his minister mother and pities his father. Kenneth's revised identity results in several changes to the backstory and the story:

1. The backstory changes because Kenneth has always been a womanizer. In the original story description Kenneth resisted Jackie's advances because he loved Mary and was faithful to her. The revised Kenneth carried on a two-year affair with Jackie while he was dating Mary, and when he broke it off he told Jackie it was because Mary was more of a woman than she was. As a result of this change in the story, Jackie's obsession with Kenneth is made darker because he's no longer the "man of her dreams" that she never had, but a man who has used and abused her.

2. The old Kenneth married Mary because he loved her. The new Kenneth married her because she was pregnant and his mother forced him to take responsibility. The new Kenneth resents being married but he loves his children and appreciates Mary's role as their mother. He shows his consideration for her and the children by being discreet in his adulterous relationships.

3. Kenneth's occupation as accountant in his mother's church introduces his parents and fellow churchgoers as supporting characters and extras in the story.

4. Kenneth's job as the church accountant, his materialism, and the resentment he feels toward his mother open up a new subplot: Kenneth has been using the church's funds in illegal activity.

5. The original story description had Kenneth falling in love with Jackie as they bond in their shared grief and guilt. The new illegal activity subplot presents another reason: Kenneth is attracted to Jackie because she can give him the money he needs to keep his business partners from harming his children.

This example, like the previous one, shows that we advanced the plot of the story by using the Character Profile Worksheet to better understand the characters. As Kenneth's character is taking shape, the story is also taking shape.

In the next example, we incorporate everything that we've learned about Roy and Kenneth into our plot outline.

EXAMPLE 8
Revised Plot Outline (*To Kill For*)

Given the new information that we now have about our story and our characters, we can revise our story description and our plot outline. I'll only show the plot outline here.

I. Chapter 1

    A. *Plot point 1–set piece: The opening.* Jackie and Roy arrive at Mary and Kenneth's for dinner.

    B. Roy confronts Jackie about his resemblance to Kenneth and begins to worry about her mental state.

    C. Kenneth meets with his business partners. Kenneth desperate.

II. Chapter 2

    A. Jackie and Mary bond.

    B. Roy visits a doctor; thinks about his mother.

    C. Jackie and Kenneth—the flirtations begin.

III. Chapter 3

    A. Mary and Kenneth argue.

    B. Jackie and Roy argue.

    C. *Plot point 2–set piece: First major story turn* (around pages 45 to 50). Mary's tragic car accident.

IV. Chapter 4

    A. Police investigation; Roy suspects Jackie.

B. Kenneth withdraws in grief and guilt.

C. Jackie insinuates herself in the lives and Kenneth and his children.

V. Chapter 5

    A. Kenneth and his business partners.

    B. Kenneth and Jackie draw closer as Jackie lies about her relationship with Roy, accusing Roy of being abusive.

    C. Roy worries about his wife.

VI. Chapter 6

VII. Chapter 7

    A. *Plot point 3—set piece: Second major story turn* (around page 100). Roy finds evidence that implicates Jackie in Mary's death.

    B. Kenneth decides to play up to Jackie because he needs her money.

VIII. Chapter 8

IX. Chapter 9

    A. Kenneth raises the pressure on the relationship with Jackie as his business partners pressure him about the money.

    B. Roy confronts Jackie and threatens to expose her.

  C. Kenneth's mother doesn't like what's going on between Jackie and Kenneth, and she's becoming suspicious about Kenneth's work at the church.

X. Chapter 10

XI. Chapter 11

  A. Kenneth's mother confronts Jackie about her relationship with Kenneth.

  B. Kenneth professes love to Jackie as business partners increase pressure on him.

  C. *Plot point 4–set piece: Third major story turn* (around page 200). Kenneth's mother is attacked; she recovers. Police question Kenneth about Mary's death.

XII. Chapter 12

XIII. Chapter 13

XIV. Chapter 14

XV. Chapter 15

  A. Jackie sees Roy with police detective.

  B. Police detective questions Jackie.

XVI. Chapter 16

XVII. Chapter 17

XVIII. Chapter 18

  A. Kenneth asks Jackie to marry him.

B. *Plot point 5–set piece: Fourth major story turn* (around page 300). Roy is attacked and goes into coma.

C. Jackie gives Kenneth the money he needs.

XIX. Chapter 19

   A. Roy comes out of his coma and asks for Kenneth. Kenneth doesn't believe Roy.

XX. Chapter 20

A. Jackie tries again to kill Roy.

XXI. Chapter 21

XXII. Chapter 22

A. Roy realizes there is nothing he can do to help Jackie.

XXIII. Chapter 23

A. *Plot point 6–set piece: The resolution* (around pages 375 to 380). Jackie's wedding and arrest.

B. Kenneth learns the truth about Mary's death.

Discussion

This plot outline is much more substantial than the plot outline previously developed, but it still needs a lot of work. My major concern is with the significance of the chosen plot point–set piece combinations. I'm not sure they are significant enough to make the story compelling. Before attempting to write the first three chapters of this story, I would complete the free-writing exercise for the new subplots introduced for Kenneth and Roy, as a way of stimulating some new ideas for the plot. In addition, I would revisit the character profiles for the two characters. I would continue to go back and forth between my characters and my plot until I felt comfortable with the plot outline and then I would start writing the first three chapters.

It is possible that after completing three chapters, I'll have to revisit my character profile and my plot again to incorporate the changes I've made while writing.

EXERCISE 11

11.1. Review the story description and plot outline that you developed in the previous chapter. Identify your least developed leading or supporting character. Use the Character Profile Worksheet to further develop that character.

11.2. List the changes the further development of your character has on your story description and plot outline.

11.3. Add any traits that you think should be added to the Character Profile Worksheet.

11.4. Delete any traits that you think should be removed from the Character Profile Worksheet.

THE CHARACTER INTERVIEW

The key to the character interview is to ask and answer enough questions to develop a well-rounded picture of your character. Of course, the interview can also be used to uncover answers to questions related to specific aspects of your character's makeup. For example, you may want to understand the character's political preferences and how those preferences play out in his daily life. Such an interview could begin with the question: What made you decide to join the Republican Party?

A powerful dynamic of the character interview is that one question asked and answered can lead to another provocative question. These spontaneous questions allow you to gain insight into your character that you may not have otherwise obtained.

The length of your interview will depend on the number and type of questions you ask. Factors influencing question selection include: the role the character plays in your story and what information you're interested in learning about the character.

In the previous chapter, I completed the free-writing and outlining exercises and began to develop the plot outline for the novella *A Gift of Love*. A review of the plot outline and story description exposes a major flaw in the story: The story is supposed to be an inspirational romance, but Jackie's faith is not intricately woven into the plot. In the following example, I use the character interview to help me answer the question, What is Jackie's faith history, and how is it interwoven in the story?

EXAMPLE 9
Character Interview (Jackie, *The Gift of Love*)

Note: The names of the main characters, James and Jackie, were changed to Kenneth and Jackie so that both names wouldn't start with the same letter.

Q: *How and when did you meet Mary and Kenneth?*
A: I met them at church about two years ago. I had

been living here in Atlanta for a couple of months and hadn't found a church that I really liked. Well, the first Sunday I went to Ebenezer I met Keelyn, their three-year-old. I sat behind the family during the service and Keelyn played peek-a-boo with me the entire time. [Jackie smiles.] When the service was over Mary, her mother, turned around and apologized to me. By that time I was smitten with little Keelyn and told Mary so. She asked if I was new and I said yes and she proceeded to introduce me to everybody. And then we talked while we waited for her husband. She wanted me to meet him too but the pastor had called a short meeting with the deacons and her husband was a deacon so we had to wait. While we waited, we talked about any and everything. I don't know. I don't usually make friends easily, but it was different with Mary. It was as if I'd known her forever.

Q: *Why do you say you don't make friends easily?*
A: Because I don't. I never have. I've always been pretty much a loner. [Jackie looks down as if she's embarrassed about this.]

Q: *Why do you think that is?*
A: I don't know really. Maybe it's because I was never around many people when I was young. You see, my mother was in her early forties when I was born and my father was in his late fifties. I was an only child. My mother didn't even think she could have kids so I was a big surprise. I think they were happy, though. [Jackie smiles again.] My mom used to say so all the time. She said she just wished that they had had me earlier so I would have had a longer time to know my father.

Q: *Is he dead?*

A: [Jackie nods and her eyes grow sad.] He died when I was in first grade. I remember he was sick all the time. And my mom was always sad. She tried to keep it from me, but even though I was a child I could sense it. I even thought it was my fault for a while. But it wasn't. My father had cancer in his lungs. My mom said it was the smoking. I don't remember him smoking, though.

Q: *Do you miss him?*

A: A lot. And my mom too. She died right before I moved here. I had moved back to my hometown after college so I could be with her. And it was a good thing I did. We had some good times together before she got sick. But after she died I needed a fresh start so I moved to Atlanta.

Q: *And what was that like?*

A: [Jackie perks up.] Until I met Mary, I think I was getting out of hand. I had started partying a lot. [She shrugged.] It seemed like a good way to meet people. But after I met Mary, I stopped partying and got involved in church activities. Since Mary liked me, everybody else seemed to like me too. I made a lot of friends, but Mary was my best friend.

Q: *What about Kenneth?*

A: [She smiles again.] I didn't know about Kenneth at first. When I first met him, I felt like he could read my mind and that he knew every sin I had ever committed. To me he was so spiritual. I didn't think he liked me at first.

Q: *What makes you think that?*
A: It's just a feeling I got. Maybe he thought I was going to be a bad influence on Mary. I thought he might stop us from becoming close friends but that didn't happen. I mentioned it to Mary once and she told me I was wrong. She said that she thought Kenneth and I were a lot alike, which is probably why I rubbed him the wrong way.

Q: *Did you think you and Kenneth were alike?*
A: No way. I told you Kenneth was this super-Christian and I was probably the most sinful person in the church. No, I didn't think Kenneth and I were anything alike. I just stayed out of his way and thanked God that Mary was still my friend.

Q: *So when did you and Kenneth become friends?*
A: [She grows sad again.] After Mary's death. I think we became a source of support for each other. Other people loved Mary, but nobody needed her the way Kenneth and I did. I guess I began to see that we were a lot alike just as Mary had said. We needed Mary in our lives because she brought out the goodness in us. Without her, we weren't sure we could make it. We did it with each other's help.

Q: *Is that why you fell in love with him?*
A: I don't really know how it happened. I just know that one day we took the twins to Discovery Zone and I looked over at him with Keelyn and Kelley and I knew that I was in love with him. I knew it just as I knew my name. It just sorta sneaked up on me. I wasn't thinking about it or anything. It was about a year after Mary's death and I was just getting used to

her not being around. And then, wham, I'm in love
with Kenneth.

Q: *I guess you didn't think that was a good thing.*
A: Of course it wasn't a good thing. My best friend
was dead. I had killed her. And there I was trying to
take over her family. The whole situation made me ill.

Q: *Is that why you went to Trinidad?*
A: That was part of it. But my life had changed a lot
after Mary's death. I don't know. I guess I wanted to
prove to her that having me for a friend wasn't a
waste. I started reading my Bible and praying and I
began to experience the love of God that Mary and I
had talked about. I learned about the church school in
Trinidad. They needed a teacher and I was available. I
thought it would be a good thing. I knew I couldn't
stay around Kenneth. I would have died if he had
found out about my feelings.

Q: *He didn't know?*
A: Thank God he didn't. He would have been as
disgusted as I was.

Q: *But hadn't you two become very good friends?*
A: Friends, yes. But he was still Mary's husband and
he was still very much in love with her.

Q: *But Mary was dead.*
A: I know that and Kenneth's head knows that but I'm
not sure his heart does. It doesn't matter anyway. He
still wouldn't be interested in me that way. We're
friends. That's all.

Q: *So did Trinidad help you get over him?*
A: Not really. Not a day passed that I didn't think
about him and the kids. I missed them so much. It was
really hard to leave the kids. We all cried.

Q: *Including Kenneth.*
A: Even Kenneth.

Q: *So what did you think when he showed up in Tobago?*
A: At first I thought something must have happened to
the kids so I was scared, but then when he told me he
came because he missed me, I got even more scared.

Q: *Why?*
A: Because it's an impossible situation. There is no
way Kenneth and I can have a future. I know that now
even more than I knew it then. You see, I should have
told Kenneth the truth about the accident. I should
have told him as soon as I woke up in the hospital.

Q: *Why didn't you tell him?*
A: [Jackie looks down again.] Because I needed him,
needed to be around him and the kids, and I knew that
if I told him he wouldn't want to see me. But I didn't
think I could live if he had shut me out of their lives. I
know now that I could but I didn't know it then.

Q: *What's changed?*
A: My faith. I now know that God would have helped
me through it. In fact, He did help me through it.

Q: *So you don't think God could help Kenneth to forgive
you?*
A: I'm not sure I want to test it. You see, Kenneth
and the kids have gone through a lot. It wouldn't be

fair to spring this on them right at the time that they're getting their lives together. This is a time for happiness, not for rehashing painful memories just so I can clear my conscience. No, this is a secret that I'm going to have to keep forever.

Q: *And that secret means you can't have a relationship with Kenneth?*
A: Exactly. We can't build a relationship on a lie and I can never tell him the truth. [She gives a dry laugh.]

Q: *What's so funny?*
A: Nothing. That wasn't a real laugh. At least, not a funny, ha-ha, laugh. I was just thinking about me and Kenneth.

Q: *What are you going to do about him?*
A: Nothing. He's only going to be here a week. He said he missed me and I miss him. I'm just going to make the best of this week. I'm going to look at it as a blessing. I won't spend my life with him, but I'm going to make the most of our time together.

Q: *What do your friends in Tobago think about him?*
A: It was love at first sight for them. They started playing matchmaker as soon as they saw him.

Q: *Do they know how you feel about him?*
A: Yes, but I didn't tell them. They've been married for more than thirty years and they say they can spot true love a mile away.

Discussion

The character interview yielded details about Jackie and her faith that I can incorporate into the plot. This new information leads to the following changes in the story and backstory:

1. The story is no longer set on a cruise ship, but on the islands of Trinidad and Tobago. The change in setting allows me to give Jackie a job as a teacher at a church school, and to introduce supporting characters as her island friends.

2. In the previous version, Jackie's fear of Kenneth's rejection was her primary motivation for keeping silent about her involvement in Mary's death. The new Jackie matured during her time away from Kenneth, and she came to realize that she should have told him the truth. Her reasons for keeping silent now are not because of her fear of rejection, but because she doesn't want to force Kenneth and his daughters to have to revisit their grief. This new reason makes the Jackie character more sympathetic, and shows the depth of her love for Kenneth and his daughters.

3. In the previous story description, Kenneth forgives Jackie for lying to him and convinces her to forgive herself and build a life with him. In this version, Kenneth forgives Jackie but he is unable to convince her to forgive herself. Jackie has to make peace with God on her own and accept the forgiveness that He offers. Once she does that, she goes to Kenneth.

The new information about the characters and the plot is reflected in the following revised plot outline for *The Gift of Love*.

EXAMPLE 10
Revised Plot Outline (*The Gift of Love*)

I. Kenneth arrives in Trinidad

   A. Kenneth at Jackie's residence; she's not there

   B. Jackie with her friends on Tobago

   C. Kenneth finds Jackie on Tobago [*the meet, plot point 1*]

II. Jackie and Kenneth with Jackie's friends—day 1

   A. Jackie takes Kenneth on a tour of the island

   B. Kenneth tells Jackie's friends about their friendship

   C. Later that night, Kenneth tells Jackie how much she helped him deal with his wife's death [*emotional intimacy, plot point 2*]

III. Jackie and Kenneth alone—day 3

   A. Kenneth's profession of love [*emotional commitment, plot point 3*]

   B. Kenneth's confusion

   C. Jackie's despair

IV. Jackie tells Kenneth her secret—day 4

   A. Jackie's confession

   B. Kenneth's anger [*the crisis, plot point 4*]

   C. Jackie and Kenneth pretend for their friends

V. Together, but separate—day 5

    A. More pretending

    B. Kenneth alone to deal with his feelings

    C. Jackie alone to deal with her feelings

VI. Kenneth and Jackie reunite—day 6

    A. Jackie's epiphany

    B. Kenneth's epiphany

    C. Reunion [*the resolution, plot point 5*]

Discussion

Clearly, this plot outline is developed more fully than the one in the previous chapter. Notice that I have moved some of the set pieces from their original positions. *The meet*, which used to open the book, is now at the end of chapter 1. I moved it because I wanted to show Jackie's and Kenneth's frame of mind when they were apart.

I would feel comfortable starting to write the book from this plot outline. Be aware, though, that a well-developed plot outline doesn't guarantee a successful story. You may make significant changes to the story as you are writing it. Or after writing a few chapters you may decide that the story doesn't work as well as you thought it would. A well-developed plot outline merely increases the probability that the story will work. It doesn't guarantee it.

EXERCISE 12

12.1. Review your developing story description and plot outline.

12.2. What questions would you like to answer about your characters?

12.3. Use the character type, character profile, or character interview to better define each character and answer those open questions.

12.4. Complete the free-writing exercise for any supporting plots that you introduce.

FIVE

DON'T GUESS, RESEARCH!

〜〜〜〜〜〜〜〜〜〜〜〜〜〜〜〜〜〜〜〜〜〜〜〜〜〜〜〜〜〜

When I decided to become a writer, I subscribed to Writer's Digest, *joined writers' groups, attended conferences and read books on plot, character development and setting.*

—Anita Bunkley (author of *Girlfriends*),
Essence magazine, 1997

As we discussed in the last two chapters, developing your plot and creating your characters are related and iterative tasks. During this process of planning your story, you'll more than likely have to reach beyond your experience for information. In technical writing terms, that means you'll have to do some research. Often new writers think of research only in the context of historical novels or novels set in exotic locales. While historical novels and exotic settings demand research, so do contemporary stories that take place in local settings. As a writer, you'll find that you have to do some research with every story. Some of your questions will be easily answered with a quick search on the Internet or a trip to your local library. Other questions will require that you expend more energy. In this chapter, we'll talk about the research process— what to research, when to research, how to research, and how to use your research findings in your story.

Why Do Research

We do research because we want our stories to be authentic. Have you ever read a book that contained inaccuracies? I'm sure you have. The complaints I hear most often concern historical novels. The author has the characters using things not yet invented or visiting towns not yet founded when the story takes place. Such errors occur because the writer did not sufficiently research her time period. Suppose, for example, the heroine in your 1889 historical novel enrolls in Spelman College. Most readers will read right over this inaccuracy, but the reader who's familiar with Spelman history will know that you didn't do your homework. Though Spelman was founded in 1881, as all Spelman T-shirts proclaim, the school was called Spelman Seminary in 1889. The reader who spots this error may begin to wonder what others she'll find in your story. Once the reader begins to question your credibility, she's no longer engaged in your story.

Now let's consider a contemporary example. Suppose you want to include a Spelman scene in your contemporary novel. You visited the campus a few years ago, so you feel pretty comfortable writing the scene from memory. In the scene, your heroine, a 1985 Spelman grad, returns for her fifteen-year reunion and gazes with nostalgia on her old dorm, Chadwick Hall. Unfortunately for you, Chadwick Hall was torn down in 1987. Again, the reader familiar with Spelman will know that you didn't do your homework, and she'll probably wonder what else you didn't do.

Research prevents us from making those historical and contemporary blunders. We research because we owe it to our readers to make our fiction as believable as possible. Make a commitment to yourself to always err on the side of caution. If you're not sure of a fact, look it up. It's much better to be safe now than sorry later. You don't want to jar the reader out of the fantasy of her reading experience because you were too lazy to look up basic information. That said, don't go to the other extreme and fret over every word you put on paper.

WHAT NEEDS RESEARCH

Story research needs tend to fall into one of several general categories. These categories include, but are not limited to: locations and settings, time periods, occupations, medical conditions and legal procedures, customs and cultures, groups and organizations, and family dynamics.

Locations and Settings

As writers we must take special care with our settings. If your story is set in a real location, you can bet that someone who lives there or someone who has visited there will read your story and quickly discover whether you did your homework. It's important to know the climate, the landscape, the governing structure, and the population demographics of the locales in your stories. Using fictional locations doesn't eliminate the need for research because fictional towns are situated around real locales. So while readers won't be able to find inaccuracies in your description of your fictional town, they may discover them because of their knowledge of the general area in which your fictional town is situated. If you set your story in southwest Arizona, your middle-class family should not live in a two-story brick house with a basement. In southwest Arizona, most homes are stucco and few, if any, have basements. For good measure, you should consider adding a pool.

Readers frequently comment that many of the stories they read could take place "anywhere," meaning that the writers didn't establish a sense of place for them. A story set in Atlanta could very well be set in San Francisco or Dallas. Suppose you set your story in the Boston area. No problem. During one of your scenes, a Dorchester resident goes to the store to buy "a soda." Big problem. Soft drinks may be referred to as sodas in Atlanta, but they are "tonics" in much of the Boston area. This inaccuracy won't ruin your story for most readers, but the reader who knows Boston won't get a Boston "feel" when she reads your work and she may begin to question your credibility. More importantly, you, the writer, will have missed a great opportunity to give your readers an authentic reading experience.

Time Periods

It's clear that when we set our stories in time periods other than today, we need to do research to make sure events are presented as they happened or would happen during the chosen time periods. You wouldn't set a story in 1980 with a character driving a Saturn—Saturns weren't manufactured until the 1990s.

Occupations

Many writers fail to research occupations adequately. One of my books, *Between the Lines*, was set around a small-town newspaper. As part of my research effort, I visited the newspaper office in a small town near my home, interviewed the editor, and observed in the newsroom for a couple of days. Surprisingly, the most valuable part of that visit was not the interview, but the observation. Watching the reporters and listening to their conversations gave me the material I needed to make the newspaper office in my book come alive. For example, I overheard staffers repeat an oft-mentioned truth about sports writing: Sports is entertainment, not brain surgery. Because I liked the phrase so much, I included a humorous scene in my story in which my heroine quoted it to the hero after he'd been assigned to cover a high school sporting event. My hard work was rewarded with a letter from a reader, a journalist, who commented that she was impressed with how accurately I had captured the journalist's life.

I've been caught not doing my research and I don't want to repeat that experience. I set one of my stories around a small-town magazine and received a letter from a reader, a magazine features writer, who commented that the magazine details were off. She even offered to provide me with accurate information if I chose to set another story around a magazine. I certainly felt badly after reading that letter. A part of me wanted to remind the reader that the story was fiction, and that as a writer I was free to take literary license. That would have been the wrong move. The reader was willing to suspend reality and engage in a fiction story, but she needed her fiction grounded in reality. My job was to ground her and I didn't do it.

Medical Conditions and Legal Procedures

Your safest bet is to verify all medical and legal information you include in your story. Don't fancifully prescribe medical remedies for your sick characters, or legal advice for your clients in trouble with the law. For one thing, medical and legal professionals as well as informed readers will know that you're bluffing. Second, believe it or not, you'll have readers who'll try those remedies and take that advice. Yes, they should know better but many times they don't. Readers can become so involved in our stories, and our characters become so real to them, that they look on the characters and the author as friends and confidants. You owe it to these readers to get your facts straight.

Customs and Cultures

Many stories have generic characters set in generic cities because the writers haven't gathered enough information to make the characters and settings unique. Research into the cultural customs and local observances of your settings will give them an authentic feel. For example, a summertime story set in Chicago might include a scene set in Grant Park for the annual Taste of Chicago festival. Alternatively, a story set in a small, rural Alabama community might include the obligatory church scene with women decked out in hats and heels, waving fans and shouting Amen to the preacher's cadenced rhymes of fire and brimstone, love and mercy.

Groups and Organizations

Groups and organizations are a wonderful way of involving your characters in the communities in which they live. You need to be familiar with the different groups and their membership requirements and demographics to use them effectively. I've had success using sororities and fraternities in my stories. I have a ready source of information in my brother and his wife, both actively involved in Greek organizations. A couple of my heroes have been fraternity members, allowing me to play on the social and professional networking opportunities provided by membership. The fraternity angle gave me an avenue for comic relief in one story. The hero, a member of the Alpha Phi Alpha fraternity, was given what-for by his frat brother's Alpha Kappa Alpha wife because he brought a Delta date to the annual fraternity picnic. More than one reader wrote to tell me how much she enjoyed the fraternity-sorority rivalries in that story.

Family Dynamics

We all grew up in families of one kind or another, but we didn't all have the same experiences. Unless all of your characters grew up in neighborhoods similar to yours, you may find yourself needing to understand the inner workings of some unfamiliar territory. For example, you may need to understand the pressures faced by a single parent or the loneliness felt by a widower. Many times we have direct resources in our lives for this kind of information; we just have to use them.

WHEN TO RESEARCH

Some stories will demand that you do research before you begin writing chapter 1. You'll need to do that when you're setting your story in an unfamiliar locale, or when a character takes on an occupation that's new to you, or when the science that supports the idea for your story is new. If you're writing about an area, location, time period, or event about which you have no direct experience, your best bet is to do some preliminary research before you plan your book. You do not want to plot a book set in north Georgia, give commercial pecan farming a crucial role, and later find out that there are no commercial pecan farms in north Georgia. Do your research up front and you'll avoid this problem altogether.

Recall the *Gift of Love* novella set in Trinidad and Tobago. Other than the white sand beaches in Tobago, the specifics of the Trinidad and Tobago locale have little impact on the plot of the story. I could have built my plot around Carnival, a nationwide party taking place two days before Ash Wednesday. The Carnival influence would change the tone of the story, and the time of year. Or the story could have taken place during the school session and showed the heroine interacting with students representative of the different cultures and social classes on the islands.

While I think that doing research up front is your best bet, there are times when you can fold your research findings into the second and subsequent drafts of your manuscript. When I started my second book, *For All Time*, I didn't know how long it took to drive from Atlanta to Raleigh, North Carolina. I didn't consider this information crucial to my plot, but surprisingly, the drive time became a major issue. The lead characters in this book were a couple in a commuter marriage, making mode of travel and travel time between the two cities of great consequence. I had to balance their financial situation with the travel time and make judicious decisions about when it made sense for them to drive and when it made sense for them to fly. It seems trivial, but the dynamics of my story changed as a result.

There is a class of research questions that you can't answer beforehand. These are the questions that arise as you're writing your story. For example, as you're writing a scene describing what the protagonist sees out of her kitchen window, you might need to know what types of flowers bloom in Maine in the springtime. When questions like these arise, you have to decide if you need the answers immediately or if you can wait until later drafts to get them. If you decide that you can wait for the answer, start a list of questions that you need answered. If you decide that you need the answer before you can proceed with the story, then stop and do your research.

How to Conduct Research

There are many methods of researching and you'll probably find that you already know and use many of them. In this section, we'll discuss some of the most frequently used methods.

Contacting Your Reference Librarian

As a writer, you should be on a first-name basis with your local reference librarian and her name should be at the top of your holiday card list. The reference librarian will become your most valuable resource. She will not know the answers to all your questions, but she'll be able to help you find the appropriate resources. Reference librarians aren't valued for the facts they know but for knowing where to find the facts.

Conducting Individual Interviews

Interviewing a person who has first-hand knowledge of your subject area is one of the most effective research methods. The interview allows you to get factual information about a subject, as well as subjective information from the interviewee's perspective. You will find these perspectives helpful when building characters. You may even choose to have one of your characters adopt the perspective of one or more of the people you interview. For example, you could interview the superintendent of your local school system and learn that he supports the local teachers group's position on teacher competency exams. After hearing the superintendent's position, you may choose to have your character take a similar position on the issue.

The keys to successful interviewing are professionalism and preparation. Professionalism demands that you be honest and forthright about your needs. Tell the interviewee your goals for the interview and describe your information needs. If the interviewee feels incapable of providing the information, ask him to refer you to a more appropriate source. By making your goals known up front, you prevent yourself and the interviewee from wasting time.

Professionalism also requires you to schedule the interview at a convenient time for the interviewee. If you plan to tape the interview, ask permission to do so when you schedule the interview. Finally, be on time. Don't make someone who is doing you a favor wait for you.

Preparation means that you arrive at the interview with your background research completed and your questions ready. If possible, you should send your questions along before the interview so that your subject can prepare too. Do not ask the interviewee questions that can be easily answered with a short trip to the library. The purpose of the interview is to collect data that you cannot get from other resources. For example, you may want to interview a policeman because you want to know what life is like for a recently married cop. You don't need to interview a police officer to find out the schedule for traffic court. An interview would be appropriate if you wanted to know how a policeman prepares for traffic court or how he feels about having to attend traffic court on his scheduled days off.

Be friendly during the interview, but don't linger after your questions have been answered. Always ask the interviewee about availability for follow-up questions. Additional questions will arise after you've had a chance to reflect on the answers you've collected. Many times these follow-up questions can be addressed in a short telephone call or an e-mail message. Ask the interviewee which mode he or she prefers.

Conducting Group Interviews

Group interviews provide a quick way of getting multiple perspectives on your questions. Interviewing groups is also a good way to observe organizational dynamics. Small groups of about four to six people tend to provide a balance of diverse perspectives and the interaction is still manageable. The rules of professionalism and preparation apply to group interviews just as they do to individual interviews.

Conducting Formal and Informal Observations

The time I spent at the newspaper is an example of a formal observation. Though I did not interact with the people that I observed, everyone in the newsroom knew who I was and why I was there. Anytime you obtain permission to observe individuals or events, the observation is considered a formal observation. These observations are scheduled just as interviews are scheduled and the rules of professionalism and preparation apply. It's a good idea to schedule an interview before and after a formal observation. I interviewed the editor of the newspaper before and after I did my observations in the newsroom. Beforehand, the editor set my expectations for what I would see during the observation. Afterward, I had the opportunity to validate my interpretation of what I had seen.

Visiting the courthouse and watching a trial in progress is an example of an informal observation. Your presence may be noted, but the reason for your presence is unknown to those being observed. When conducting informal observations, you must be careful not to infringe on people's privacy. A good litmus test is to ask yourself how you would feel being observed in a similar situation.

Visiting Settings and Locations

Visiting a location is the most authentic way to experience it and will yield a rich set of data to use in your story. Taking a video recorder along on research trips allows you to cover more ground in less time, since you won't have to write down all of your observations. You still will have to take notes on the smells, feels, and sounds that can't be captured on videotape.

While research travel is effective (many times even tax deductible!), it can quickly become quite expensive; therefore you should choose your research trips carefully. If you can't visit a locale of interest, call the chamber of commerce, visitors center, or library in the area and tell them what information you need and why. Many times they will have brochures or videos that you'll find helpful.

Reading Books and/or Watching Videos

You can check out a book or rent a video about almost any subject. Don't overlook this valuable source of information. Be sure to verify that the books and videos you use correspond to the time period of your story. A video on herbal medicines done in the nineties probably won't be appropriate for research on a story set in the sixties. Travel guides, like Fodor's, are also good sources. Again, make sure they are current to the time period of your story.

Searching the Internet

The Internet is a ready source of information on almost any topic. Search engines and search directories like Yahoo (www.yahoo.com), Lycos (www.lycos.com), and WebCrawler (www.webcrawler.com) will locate information by subject or keyword. The more you restrict your search parameters, the more likely the search results will be valuable to you. A search on *Georgia pecan farming* will result in a much more manageable list of Web pages than a search on *farming* or a search on *pecan farming*. Internet searching is more an art than a science, so you'll often use the trial and error method of selecting search terms.

Don't forget about Internet discussion groups, also called newsgroups or Usenet groups. Discussion groups exist for most any topic you can name. Have a question about consulting? Search the group alt.misc.consulting. Use the discussion group search engine Dejanews (www.dejanews.com) to search newsgroups. You'll find discussion group readers very willing to answer your questions. Online services like AOL, Prodigy, or CompuServe have internal discussion groups, called bulletin boards and forums. Pop into one with a question and you're bound to get a response. Before posting a question to a newsgroup, check its FAQ (Frequently Asked Questions) file. Your question may be one that's commonly asked.

The major downside to Internet research is determining the credibility of the information you find. Suppose you want to set your story on one of the Sea Islands off the Georgia coast. A Yahoo search returns a listing of sites that match your criteria, including the Web page of a family living on one of the islands. On their page you find a detailed description of their life in the islands. The information seems to be exactly what you're looking for, but how do you know it's accurate? Unfortunately, there is no content verifier on the Internet and people are free to post any information they like. While there are sites designed to intentionally mislead Internet surfers, there are more well-intentioned sites with information that is incomplete, out-of-date, biased, or just plain wrong. Therefore, caution is the word to remember when doing Internet research. Verify any information you collect from the Internet with two or more sources.

The Internet proved a great resource of information on Trinidad and Tobago. Using Yahoo I found an organization involved in a project to promote a sister city relationship between Atlanta, Georgia, and Port of Spain, Trinidad. Then I visited a local discussion group and "met" Trinidad natives. Finally, I used e-mail to arrange a meeting with one of the Trinidad natives who lived in my local area.

Reading Craft and Genre Magazines

General writing magazines like *Writer's Digest* and *The Writer* can serve as good research sources. Often they contain research articles and list research resources. Genre specific publications, like Romance Writers of America's *Romance Writers Report*, the American Crime Writers League's *BUL-LETin*, and the Science Fiction Writers of America's *Bulletin*, often contain genre-specific research articles. Although these trade magazines rarely give the kind of detail you need for your story, they usually include a bibliography of reference works that you can use for more detailed study. Black literary magazines, like *American Visions*, *Quarterly Black Review of Books*, and *Black Issues Book Review*, are excellent sources of up-to-date information on the book business from the black perspective. In addition to book reviews, the magazines also feature author interviews and publishing industry updates.

How to Use Your Research in Your Story

The key point to remember when you have all your glorious research in front of you is that you don't have to, and probably shouldn't try to, use all of it in your story. Treat your research findings as a well of information from which to draw for your current and future books. Some information you'll use in your current project, and never again; some you'll incorporate into your current book and in one or more future books; other information you will never use at all. Always remember that your research findings should be used to tell your story; your story should not be an outlet to dump research findings.

EXAMPLE 11
Research Questions (*To Kill For*)

Recall the plot outline that we developed for the suspense novel *To Kill For*. Research could answer some of the open questions related to the story. A listing of a few of those questions follow. The brackets following each question enclose a suggested research method. In addition, a BEFORE tag is included to indicate research that I should conduct before I start writing the book.

1. Location and settings: Where in Atlanta does the story take place? What can I use to uniquely characterize this location? [BEFORE: Atlanta Chamber of Commerce]

2. Occupations: What occupations should I assign to the leading and supporting characters to best enhance the plot of the story? [BEFORE: Newspaper want ads, library jobs digest]

3. Medical: What causes a coma? What are its characteristics? How is it treated? What is the prognosis? [Internet search]

4. Legal: What is the common procedure for investigating an automobile accident that results in a fatality? [BEFORE: Interview a police detective]

5. Customs/culture: How are funerals handled? What's the norm for mourning? [Telephone interview with a funeral director local to the area]

6. Groups and organizations: What organizational affiliations can I assign to the leading and supporting characters to best enhance the plot of the story? [BEFORE: library]

7. Family dynamics: How common are women pastors? How are they perceived in the local society of the story setting? [BEFORE: Internet discussion group]

EXERCISE 13

13.1. This chapter provides the following "What Needs Research" categories: locations and settings, time periods, occupations, medical conditions and legal procedures, customs and cultures, groups and organizations, and family dynamics. Using these categories to stimulate your thinking, identify the research needs in the plot outline and character descriptions that you created for exercise 12.2.

13.2. Now create your personal list of "What Needs Research" categories. This list should include the categories described in this chapter and categories you create to fulfill your particular project's needs. Build on this list and keep it for use with future books.

13.3. For each item you've identified as needing research in exercise 13.2, decide whether the research should be done *before* you begin writing your manuscript or if it can wait until the second or subsequent drafts. Create two lists: one, the "Before" list, with the items needing research before you start writing your book; the other with the items you can follow up on later.

13.4. This chapter provides the following "How to Research" methods: library, interviews, observations, visits, books and videos, Internet, and writing magazines. For each item you've identified as needing research in exercise 13.2, jot down the *research method* that you plan to use to obtain the information. Feel free to include research methods not listed here.

13.5. Create your personal "research method" list. This list should include the methods described in this chapter and any methods that you identified in 13.3. Build on this list and keep it for use with future books.

13.6. Do your research for the items on your "Before" list.

13.7. After completing your research, update your character descriptions and plot outline to reflect what you've learned.

SIX

WHOSE POINT OF VIEW IS IT?

〜〜〜〜〜〜〜〜〜〜〜〜〜〜〜〜〜〜〜〜〜〜

As an emerging writer I cast around quite a bit looking for my voice, that authority that rings with truth, that makes each writer's work her own. As I continued to do the work (the writing, the discipline, the reading, the thinking) I realized that I talked a great deal about my mother. I assumed all women did. Perhaps that is why I had not noticed for all these years that my mother's center is exactly from whence my voice as a writer first sprang. It is a voice that speaks not just with clever words, but also with authority, wisdom, wit and truth.

—Tina Ansa (author of *And You Should Know Better*), *Essence* magazine, 1995

Point of view (POV) refers to the *eyes* through which the writer, and thus the reader, views the story or particular scene. The eyes belong to the POV character. Writing a scene in a particular character's POV means that only what that character sees, hears, smells, tastes, feels, and thinks is presented in the scene. The reader, by extension, can only experience what that character experiences.

Suppose, for example, an accountant sneaks up behind a private investigator (PI) searching through his office files. If the accountant is the POV character, the writer can give the reader direct access to what the accountant is thinking, doing, seeing, saying, and feeling, but the reader can only know what the PI is doing or saying indirectly through the accountant. If the PI is removing folders from the filing cabinet and tossing them on the desk, the reader won't know it until the accountant sees it.

If the PI is the POV character, the writer can give the reader direct access to his thoughts and actions, but the reader can only have indirect access to the thoughts and actions of the accountant. The reader will learn the accountant is in the room when the PI realizes he's there, making the accountant's presence as much a surprise to the reader as it is to the PI.

Some writers refer to writing from a specific character's POV as being *inside that character's head*. When writing from a character's POV, the author is free to reveal the character's thoughts. If there are two characters in a scene, the writer should give only the thoughts of the POV character. Consider the previous example with the PI as the POV character. In this situation, only the PI's thoughts should be presented. The reader cannot know the accountant's thoughts because the writer is not inside the accountant's head, the accountant is not the POV character. The only information the writer can reveal about the accountant is what the PI observes about him, thinks about him, or feels about him.

First-person—or "I"—POV and limited third-person POV are commonly used in fiction. In first-person POV, the story is told through the eyes of a single character, the narrator, who talks directly to the reader. First-person POV is often found in mysteries in which the POV character is the sleuth who's trying to solve the crime. In first-person POV stories, the entire book, not just a scene, is told from the narrator's perspective. Consider the following example of the start of a first-person story:

> I didn't know what to think when I walked into the dank,
> smoke-filled room. Jack was drinking, my head was hurting,
> and all I wanted to do was scream.

The "I" character, or narrator, participates in the story and is telling the story.

The limited third-person POV allows the story to be told from the POV of multiple characters, usually the lead characters. The advantage and popularity of the limited third-person POV is that it allows the reader to develop an intimacy with each character. Consider the following example of the beginning of a limited third-person POV scene:

> Jeffrey kicked the door shut. "Good riddance," he shouted.
> *Who died and made her boss anyway?*

Jeffrey is the POV character here. We know he is because the question "Who died and made her boss anyway?" is not something Jeffrey said, but something he thought.

A less commonly used POV is the omniscient POV. In this POV, the scene is told through the eyes of a narrator who is not a character in the story. The narrator, who sees all and knows all, views the action of the story as a bystander. The advantage of the omniscient POV is that the reader is allowed to get inside the heads of many characters, and the author can make commentary that none of the characters in the story would make. The disadvantage is that the reader has a more difficult time bonding with the characters. Consider the following example of the omniscient POV, from Toni Morrison's *Beloved*.

> The couple upstairs, united, didn't hear a sound, but below
> them, outside, all around 124 the snow went on and on and
> on. Piling itself, burying itself. Deeper. Higher.

In this passage, the narrator knows and is able to tell what the couple upstairs hears, as well as what's going on outside below them.

The omniscient POV can be used effectively by skilled writers, but less skilled writers may find it difficult to execute it effectively.

Effective Use of Limited Third-Person POV

The most effective use of the limited third-person POV is to restrict each story scene to a single POV *unless* there is a compelling reason to switch. Sticking with a single POV character requires discipline. It forces the writer to think through each story scene in detail to find its most effective structure and presentation.

There will be times when you want the reader to know what both characters in the scene are thinking and the easiest way to do that is to switch from the POV of one character to the POV of the other character. A much more difficult way to accomplish your goal would be to structure the story scene so that the reader has direct access to one character's thoughts (the POV character). The other character's thoughts are shown indirectly through the eyes and thoughts of the POV character as he reads other characters' facial expressions and body language.

Effective use of POV begins with effective selection of the POV character. Before you begin writing each story scene, you should select a character whose perspective you plan to take for the entire story scene. If an occasion arises when you want to switch POV within the story scene, you have three options:

1. Switch to the new POV character, signaling this switch by starting a new book scene, and stay with the

new POV for the remainder of the story scene or for a reasonably large segment of it.

2. Switch to a new POV character for an exchange or two *without* starting a new book scene.

3. Switch back and forth between the POV of multiple characters in the scene without starting a new book scene.

The three options differ in three key ways: the length of the passage dedicated to a single POV character, the frequency of POV changes, and the use of a scene break to signal the change in POV. In the first option, the length of the passage is long, covering an entire conversation or movement of your story scene. POV changes after long passages can be effectively signaled with a scene break.

In the second option, one character's POV carries most of the scene, with infrequent short breaks into the POV of other characters—maybe just one or two dialogue exchanges or a paragraph of introspection. Using scene breaks to signal POV changes after short passages would prove unwieldy.

The third option, sometimes called *head-hopping*, is an exaggeration of the second. In this option, no POV dominates the scene; rather, there are frequent shifts in POV among any, or all, of the characters in the scene. I advise against head-hopping because you run the risk of your readers not bonding with your characters, and if your readers don't bond with your characters, they will lose interest in your story. Of course, you will find stories that seem to employ head-hopping as a stylistic tool. While the technique won't detract from some stories, it can kill others.

Some writers are POV purists who contend that there is never a good reason to change POV in a story scene. These writers would not recommend any of the three options. Obviously, I'm not one of those writers. While the first option is my preferred method, there are times when I use the second. My basic position is that you only use the second option when you have a compelling reason to do so.

Let's look at a few passages written in the limited third-person POV.

> "Have a seat, my boy," Mr. Sanders said. He walked over to the eight-foot upholstered couch that stretched in front of the idle brick fireplace. "How do you like our town so far?"
>
> Jake's thoughts went immediately to the woman he'd seen in the pool. He liked her, but he couldn't tell Mr. Sanders that. "It's certainly not New York."
>
> Mathias Sanders laughed, a rich full laugh that deepened the wrinkles around his eyes and mouth. "You're right about that, but give us a chance. Lamar is not such a bad place."

We know that Jake is the POV character in this passage because we hear his thoughts in the second paragraph. Though Mathias Sanders does most of the talking and, indeed, he dominates the passage, it is as if the reader were observing it all through Jake's eyes.

Let's look a little more closely at what we learn about Mathias. First, we hear him speak and we see him cross the room. We see and hear this because Jake, who's already in the room, sees and hears it. Next, we hear Mathias laugh a full laugh and we see the wrinkles about his eyes become more pronounced when he does. We hear the laughter as "full" because Jake heard it and characterized it as such. If there were a third person, say, a woman, in the room and she was the POV character, she may have characterized Mathias's laughter another way. In this passage, we are seeing, hearing, and experiencing what Jake is seeing, hearing, and experiencing. Everything in the passage is from Jake's point of view, or Jake's perspective.

Let's continue on. We know the wrinkles around Mathias's

eyes grow more pronounced when he laughs because Jake sees it. Mathias couldn't see it himself unless he had a mirror. He may be able to feel it but he could not reveal it to the reader because he is not the POV character. Once Jake was chosen as the POV character, the decision was made for the reader to learn about all the characters in the scene through Jake's senses and thoughts.

What do we learn about Jake in this passage? First, we observe that though he is talking to Mathias, his thoughts are with a woman he met by a pool. From his thoughts, we learn that he likes the woman and that he doesn't think it appropriate to discuss her with Mathias. Our direct access to Jake's thoughts gives us this information.

What else do we know about Jake? We know that he's observant. When Mathias enters the living room, we see what Jake sees: an eight-foot upholstered couch. What if Jake had had a different impression of the couch? Consider the following revised passage:

> "Have a seat, my boy," Mr. Sanders said. He walked over to the battered sofa, which looked as though a dog had slept on it last night. "How do you like our town so far?"

It's obvious in this revised passage that Jake is seeing a different sofa than the one he saw in the original passage. The point that I'm emphasizing here is that the reader sees the scene as Jake, the POV character, sees it.

Sometimes a writer will expand on passages like these to give more detail about the setting. Instead of a single sentence with brief descriptions of how Jake sees the couch and the fireplace, the writer will add a long paragraph that fully describes the entire living room. There is nothing inherently wrong with describing a room in such detail, but the POV character must have a reason for cataloging the contents of the room.

There could be a good reason. Is the POV character an interior decorator who routinely takes note of room layouts as part of her job? Or is the room so horrid that the POV character is compelled to take in its every detail? Or is the room filled with such expensive furnishings that the POV character, who has never had more than ten dollars in his pocket, can't believe he's standing in the middle of such wealth? Or does the room hold sentimental value to the POV character and as he looks at each item, he shares the memory the item holds for him? Consider the following example:

> Jake couldn't stand being in this room. It hurt too much. He still remembered the day they had bought that stupid red couch. He'd thought it was the ugliest thing in the department store, but she'd loved it. He'd brought it home with a smile because he had never been able to deny her anything.

In this passage we get another view of the couch through Jake's eyes. The description is not provided merely to inform the reader that there is a red couch in the room; the reader also learns Jake's history, his current state of mind, and the sentimental value the couch has for him. If the author so chose and the story dictated, the passage could continue on around the room, describing all of its contents as they relate to Jake's state of mind.

Effective Use of First-Person POV

Effective use of first-person POV begins with effective selection of the POV character, in this case, the narrator. This narrator should be the character the story is about. The reader will be allowed into the head of this single character, so choose him wisely. As I said before, the POV character should be the character that you want the reader to know most intimately and the character with the greatest insight into what's happening in your story.

You'll find first-person POV stories told from the perspective of what seems like one of the supporting characters, but a closer investigation will reveal that the supporting character is, in fact, a lead character in the story. The major action of the story may not include this character, but it impacts him most. In such cases, the heart of the story is not the big event but the response to that big event.

Let's look now at a first-person POV passage from Evelyn Coleman's *What a Woman's Gotta Do.*

The woman who sat next to me squirmed, her short jet-black hair sprouting blond roots. She had walked in with black manicured nails with white pelicans painted in the center. But at the rate she was chewing on them, the lower halves of the pelicans were surely crippled by now. And she would leave with not only varying sizes of silver and turquoise rings on each finger, but bloody nubs.

The tattooed man with her, his shoulder-length hair also dyed jet black, kept saying, "Damn, you gone bite your hand off before we even get in there."

The engagement ring on her finger made me wonder if Tattoo Man might have a pocket full of bubble gum, since I was reasonably sure the ring didn't pop out on the first try.

By 4:10 p.m. when Kenneth still had not shown, I asked Tattoo Man and Biting Nails, "Excuse me. Got any chewing gum?" Despite the tears stinging at the corners of my eyes, I almost burst into laughter when he pulled out a handful of colorful balls.

"Look, don't take the red ones. They're mine," he said.

I don't suppose he noticed that his sweating hands and funked-up pockets had turned the red ones pink and speckled gray. I shook my head and said, "Thanks anyway, I can't chew bubble gum." I pointed to my top teeth—"Dentures"—

hoping that this small lie would gross him out and he'd move back.

The POV character in this scene is the "I" character, Patricia Conley, the story's protagonist. It's clear that Patricia is the POV character because every thought and action in the passage is presented from her POV. There are two other people in the scene but all we know about them is what Patricia observes. We know about the woman's dyed hair, nail-biting habit, and cheap-looking (at least in Patricia's eyes) engagement ring. We know that the tattooed man is with her and that he also has dyed hair. We hear a bit of their conversation because Patricia hears it.

We also learn something about Patricia from this passage. We learn about her attention to detail—not surprising since she's a journalist—as evidenced in her observations of the man and woman. We can infer that she's quick-witted and probably has an acerbic sense of humor because of the nicknames she assigns to the man and woman, her speculation about the origin of the woman's engagement ring, and the way she turns down the tattooed man's offered bubble gum. Most importantly, we know that Patricia is hurting right now because Kenneth has not arrived.

As you have seen in this chapter, point of view can be a powerful writer's tool. The questions in the following exercise will help you to develop your skill with POV.

EXERCISE 14

14.1. Which POV do you see most often in the books you read?

14.2. Select a book scene from a book that's written in first-person POV and answer the following questions:

14.2.1. Who is the POV character?

14.2.2. Why do you think that character was chosen as the narrator?

14.2.3. What do you learn about the character in the scene?

14.2.4. What do you learn about the other characters?

14.3. Select a book scene from a book that's written in limited third-person POV and answer the following questions:

14.3.1. Who is the POV character?

14.3.2. Why do you think that character was chosen as the POV character?

14.3.3. What do you learn about the POV character in the scene?

14.3.4. What do you learn about the other characters in the scene?

14.3.5. Does the author change POV in the book scene? If so, how many times and are the changes effective?

SEVEN

THINKING, SPEAKING, AND DOING

∿∿∿∿∿∿∿∿∿∿∿∿∿∿∿∿∿∿∿∿∿∿∿∿∿∿∿∿∿∿∿∿

I love words—their sounds, their multiple meanings and shadings, the powers we give them to teach, to wound, to build, to heal. I love discovering how other people use words. I love the sounds of words. I'm more an ear-minded person than an eye-minded one. Other writers tell me they visualize their stories on imaginary screens or stages. I hear mine as "radio plays." I fashion dialogues to ease my characters into situations that feel unfamiliar or uncomfortable to me. I'm addicted to specialized dictionaries of science, religion, history, names, medicine, law.

—Octavia Butler
(author of *Wild Seed*),
Essence magazine, 1995

If you have done your research and invested sufficient time developing your characters and your plot outline, you probably have more information than you can ever use in your story. Your challenge and the challenge for most writers is deciding what to include and the most effective way to include it. We will use the phrase *reveal character* to denote this process of including character information in a story; the phrase is appropriate because it characterizes how relationships are formed.

Upon meeting a new person, most of us don't launch into

our life story. Instead, we reveal ourselves in bits and pieces as we feel safe doing so in the relationship. There are a couple of reasons why most of us naturally do this. First, you don't want to bore the other person. Think about it: You meet someone and immediately she starts telling you her life story. You've just met this person. Are you really that interested? Second, suppose you *are* interested in the person. How much of her life story are you going to remember if she dumps it all on you at your first meeting? Very little. Third, a little mystery can liven up a relationship. Can you imagine knowing all there is to know about a person after the first meeting? What would be the point of seeing her again? Fourth, everything in your life doesn't need to be told. What's the point of telling someone that you stubbed your toe in second grade? Everybody did. Unless you stubbed yours against a rattlesnake that then bit and almost killed you, your toe-stubbing incident should probably be relegated to the file of things not worth mentioning.

These four reasons are also the reasons you don't want to dump all the information you have about your characters on the first page of your story, or in the first chapter. First, you don't want to bore your reader by telling her a lot of facts about your character when your story first opens. Second, the reader is not going to remember all of the information anyway so you will have to repeat some of it or the reader will have to continually flip back to the early pages of the story to refresh her memory. Third, the reader likes some mystery. If she knows all there is to know about the character in chapter 1, why should she keep reading? And fourth, the reader's only interest is in the events of the character's life that relate to the story being told. Don't confuse her by including irrelevant or unnecessary information.

Your goal as the writer is to reveal your characters over the course of your story. Fortunately, there are tools and techniques to help you achieve this goal. Two tools—dialogue and interior monologue—and a pair of techniques—*showing* and *telling*—will be presented in this chapter. *Dialogue* refers to the words the characters speak aloud; *interior monologue* refers to the thoughts the characters think; and *showing* and *telling* refers to putting your characters in action and allowing your readers to get to know them by their actions.

DIALOGUE

In simple terms, dialogue is what your characters say, but for writers dialogue is more than characters speaking words. Dialogue is characters speaking words *with a purpose*. In fiction, dialogue usually serves two purposes: to reveal character and to advance plot.

How can dialogue reveal character? Imagine yourself meeting a new person. What do you think of that person if all he talks about is himself? What do you think if he uses profanity every other word? What if he speaks in a monotone? Though you may not know much about a person, you draw conclusions about his character and personality based on what he says and how he says it. Four lines of dialogue may not tell you a lot about a character, but it can hint at a great deal. Writers build characterizations from many dialogues, some no longer than a mere four lines.

The dialogue used by a character helps the reader form a picture of the character. Therefore, the writer should use dialogue effectively to make sure the reader forms an accurate picture. Some characters curse all the time; others never curse. Some characters use slang; others don't. Some characters use dialect; others don't. Readers draw conclusions about characters based on the way they speak. As a writer you must constantly ask yourself what conclusions you want the reader to draw about your characters.

You also must consider carefully what your characters say

and when they say it. All conversation in your story must serve some story purpose. Would you include the conversation your lead character has with the gas station attendant as he pays for his gas? Only if it were important to the story. If your guy is normally very friendly to the gas station attendant but on this day he's distracted by other things, you may want to include the conversation because it shows his state of mind. On the other hand, if the conversation is of standard fare— "Pump three." "That'll be $15.25." "Wait. Let me give you a quarter with that." "Thank you"—you might be wise to leave it out.

If you are to write effective dialogue, there are a few other points you must consider. First, readers should be able to distinguish the individual voices of your characters. Just as you as a writer have a voice that is revealed in your stories, each of your lead characters should have a readily identifiable voice. Again, voice doesn't only refer to sound, but also to word usage and style. Compare the *voice* of Democrat Jesse Jackson to the *voice* of Republican J. C. Watts. Their voices have a similar tonal quality but their use of words and their cadences are distinctly different. As Democrats and Republicans, it goes without saying that they often have different views about the same issue.

Second, your characters should use contractions when they speak, since most people do. If you have a character who doesn't use contractions, there must be a reason and that reason must be communicated to the reader. Only the most formal of characters, or characters pretending to be formal, speak without using contractions. Of course, not using contractions could be a character quirk. For example, in order to fit in at an elite country club, your nouveau riche heroine might adopt a false formality in her speech.

Third, dialogue must sound as though people are really speaking. Dialogue has to be real. It must sound as though the character is talking and not as though you, the writer, are preaching or lecturing to the reader. One way to check for realism in your dialogue is to read it aloud. Does it sound like people talking? Be sure to watch for long passages. People don't tend to speak in long passages unless they're lecturing. Another characteristic of conversation is that people interrupt each other; this should be reflected in your dialogue as well. Don't go overboard, though; too many interruptions can be confusing for the reader. It can also be annoying. Like not using contractions, interrupting can be a character quirk. For example, your story could have an obnoxious supporting character who thinks he's the resident expert on any and all topics. A party scene could show him jumping in before anyone he talks to has a chance to finish their sentences.

Fourth, body language plays a major role in dialogue. Many times people say more with their bodies than they do with their mouths. A character slamming his fist on the table before saying "Go ahead," is quite different from a character easing down on the couch and saying the same thing. Put your characters in action as they speak, even if they only make simple gestures like nodding or raising an eyebrow. *Talking heads*, dialogue without action, can kill a story.

Many writers seem to struggle with the grammatical rules for writing dialogue. Here are a few that you should know:

1. Put dialogue in quotation marks with the punctuation *inside* the quotations. For example:

A: "Show, don't tell," he said.
B: "Did he say that?"

2. Limit the use of speaker attributions (he said, she said). If two people are speaking, it's not necessary to tell who spoke after each exchange. The reader knows. With more than two characters, the reader needs to be informed who's talking. Fortunately, identification of the

speaking character can be accomplished without speaker attributions. For example:

A: "I told you," Trevonia said.
B: Trevonia propped her hands on her hips. "I told you."

In example B we identified the speaking character by associating an action with her dialogue.

3. Be careful when using speaker attributions. Many new writers go overboard in their effort to use a word other than the commonly used *said*.

INCORRECT: "Stop it," she grunted.
CORRECT: She grunted. "Stop it."
INCORRECT: "Stop it," she grinned.
CORRECT: She grinned. "Stop it."

Grunting and grinning aren't ways of speaking; they are actions. Just because you can find examples of these words used as attributions in novels by your favorite writers doesn't mean that the words are being used correctly. You can safely use the verbs *shout, yell, whisper, scream, murmur,* and similar words as alternatives to *say* when they appropriately reflect how your characters are speaking.

4. Show, don't tell. This is where your skill as a writer can shine. You must choose the best word to show what the character is feeling. Instead of using a weak verb-adverb combination, give the reader a picture. For example:

WEAK: "Quiet," he said angrily.
STRONG: He slashed his fist through the air. "Quiet, I said."

Instead of telling the reader the character is angry, show that the character is angry by his actions.

5. Use a dash to show a character being interrupted:

"You should—"

6. Use ellipses to show a character trailing off:

"Like I was saying . . ."

7. Start a new paragraph with each new speaker. This is an indication to the reader that the speaker has changed.

As you have seen in this section, dialogue is a powerful writer's tool. The following exercise will help you develop your skill at writing dialogue.

EXERCISE 15

Write a short passage (two to four sentences) of dialogue for each of the following situations. The first one is done for you.

15.1. Eileen's boss tells her that she's been promoted. "Congratulations, Eileen," he said, when she reached him. "I know you're going to make your mark with this new job."

15.2. Eileen responds to the news that she's been promoted.

15.3. Rodney accuses his best friend, Derrick, of embezzling money from the company they jointly own.

15.4. Derrick defends himself against Rodney's accusation.

INTERIOR MONOLOGUE

One of the most powerful tools the writer can use is interior monologue, the POV character's internal conversation and thoughts. Books are the only art form that allows the thoughts of the characters to be explicitly stated. In most movies, readers must infer a character's thoughts from his facial expressions, body language, words, and actions. The exception is when a director lets us inside a character's head using voiceovers. The same goes for theater. Characters in books also use facial expressions, body language, words, and actions to convey their inner thoughts, but readers don't have to rely solely on inference to know a character's thoughts. Using interior monologue, the writer can present the character's thoughts directly on the page.

Just because the writer *can* put those thoughts directly on the page doesn't mean that the writer *should*. Readers don't need to know every thought the POV character thinks. Some thoughts are tangential or irrelevant to the story and others are so readily inferred as to make stating them redundant. Interior monologue is a tool and it's the writer's responsibility to use that tool skillfully. The writer may choose to have the character think, *Woe is me, my mother was mean to me*. Or the writer may create a scene in which the adult character has a conversation with his parent that hints at their past relationship. Or the writer may create a scene in which the character interacts with his own child in a way that hints at the relationship he had with his mother. Or the writer may create a scene where the character describes his parenting techniques as drastically different from those of his abusive parents. The options for revealing the character's relationship with his parents are limited only by the writer's imagination and the plot.

Let's look at two examples of the effective use of interior monologue. First, consider the case where the writer wants the reader to sympathize with a character who says and does things that don't seem to deserve sympathy. For example:

"Don't you dare," Jack said, slapping her for the third time. "You're not leaving me."

From this short passage, we learn that Jack is slapping a woman for the third time—not something that elicits our sympathy, right? But let's see what a little interior monologue can do for this passage:

"Don't you dare," Jack said, slapping her for the third time. She couldn't die. She just couldn't. He loved her too much. She had to wake up. She had to. "You're not leaving me."

This short passage presents a totally different picture of Jack. He is still performing the same actions but his actions are now in context. Now look at this passage:

Jack lifted the drink to his lips and took a long swallow before answering her question. "I don't love you," he finally said. "I've never loved you."

In this passage Jack comes across as cold, but what do you think a little introspection can do for his personality?

Jack lifted the drink to his lips and took a long swallow before answering her question. He was about to do the most difficult thing he'd ever done. He loved her more than he loved himself but if she stayed with him, she'd always be in danger. He loved her too much to make her live that way. "I don't love you," he finally said. "I've never loved you."

Are you beginning to understand how interior monologue can take one instance of action and dialogue and give it a different meaning?

The manuscripts of new writers many times reflect technical problems in the interior monologue. Some writers erroneously treat it like dialogue and put it in quotations:

"I just bet you would," he thought.

The passage can be correctly written in one of two ways:

I just bet you would, he thought.
I just bet you would.

The first example is written much like dialogue, except the quotation marks are omitted. In the second example, underlining the words indicates the line should be italicized in the printed book. Italics indicate to the reader that the words were thought and not spoken.

Other writers encounter POV problems when writing interior monologue because they want to tell what each character in the scene is thinking. Wrong! Limit interior monologue to the POV character.

Some writers think that you must include *wondered* or *thought* to indicate that a particular segment of text is interior monologue:

He wondered if she was upset with him.
He doesn't believe me, she thought.

While the above examples are technically correct, formating all interior dialogue this way would prove monotonous. For variety, try these styles:

He knew she was upset with him.

He didn't believe her.

As you have seen in this section, interior monologue is a powerful writer's tool. The following exercise will help you develop your skill at writing interior monologue.

EXERCISE 16

Using dialogue and interior monologue, write a short passage (four to seven sentences) describing the following situations. The first one is done for you.

16.1. Eileen's boss tells her that she's been promoted. POV character: the boss.

Walter watched her walk toward him. Just look at her, he thought. She doesn't deserve this job. Of course, he couldn't voice that truth. No, he had to tow the company line. "Congratulations, Eileen," he said, when she reached him. "I know you're going to make your mark with this new job." She was going to make her mark all right. As far as he was concerned, American productivity was dealt a bad hand when they allowed women in the workplace.

16.2. Eileen after her boss tells her that she's been promoted. POV character: Eileen.

16.3. Jackson sees his high school sweetheart, Patrice, at their twenty-year reunion. POV character: Jackson.

16.4. Patrice sees her high school sweetheart, Jackson, at their twenty-year reunion. POV character: Patrice.

SHOW, DON'T TELL

"Show, don't tell," the writer is often told. Well, what does that mean? When I was working on my first book, a published author critiqued my work and told me that I needed to "show, instead of tell." Since I had no idea what she meant, I proceeded to question her. After about ten questions, I began to nod my head though I still didn't understand what she meant. I concluded that an understanding of showing and telling would remain hidden from me until I was a more mature writer. Eight years and about nine books later, I think I finally have a handle on it.

When showing, you, the writer, are painting a picture for your reader so that she'll "see" and "feel" your story as she reads it. One way of accomplishing this is to be specific, not general. For example, *brown cocker spaniel* paints a more vivid picture than *dog*, and *rusty red VW Beetle* paints a more vivid picture than *car*. In the same way, it's more effective for a character to take deep breaths and count to ten than it is for the writer to simply say the character was annoyed.

Instead of telling the reader that a character is a good father, allow the reader to see the character interacting with his child in a positive manner. Let's look at two examples:

1. Eleanor was annoyed with John because he was late.

2. Eleanor grabbed his wrist and thumped the face of his Rolex. "Look, John," she said. "I don't know why you have to be late all the time."

The first passage is *telling*, because the reader is being told Eleanor's state of mind (she's annoyed because John was late) without any action or dialogue to support the claim. The second passage is *showing*, because Eleanor's words and her body language indicate her state of mind (she's annoyed because John was late).

While showing can be effective, it's not always appropriate. Consider the following two examples:

1. Patsy got in her car and buckled the seat belt. She put her key in the ignition and turned it. Then she put the car in reverse and looked in her rearview mirror. There was no traffic, so she backed out into the street. She put the car in drive, straightened the wheel, and headed down the street. At the first stop sign, she stopped and looked both ways to make sure the way was clear. She drove through the intersection. At the next stop sign, she stopped again . . .

2. Patsy drove home.

The first passage is clearly a *showing* passage, but does the reader need to see every move Patsy makes while driving home? Not unless her car is going to blow up when she shifts gears. In other words, giving significant detail to an insignificant event such as driving home clues the reader that something important is going to happen. If nothing is going to happen during the drive home, the second, *telling*, statement is more appropriate. As these examples show, telling is not always ineffective or inappropriate. There are some things, namely minor points in the story, that the writer *should* tell. In those cases, it is more effective to tell than it is to show.

As you have seen in this section, showing and telling are powerful writer's tools. The following exercise will help you develop your skill at using both effectively.

EXERCISE 17

In this exercise you will examine the way your favorite authors weave character information throughout their stories using dialogue, interior monologue, and effective showing and telling.

17.1. Using the Modified Character Profile Worksheet, identify the character traits the writer reveals about the lead character in the first three chapters of two books you've read recently. When you finish this exercise, look back over the worksheet to see how the information was sprinkled throughout the three chapters.

MODIFIED CHARACTER PROFILE WORKSHEET

Book title: _____

Number of pages: _____

Key:

How refers to how the information about the character is presented to the reader: internal monologue (IM), dialogue (D), showing (S), telling (T)

Who refers to the character who reveals the information: self (S), another leading character (LC), supporting character (SC), extra (E)

	How	Who	Pg
Name _____			

Physical Attributes

Sex _____			
Age _____			
Height _____			
Build _____			
Eyes _____			
Skin _____			
Hair _____			
Speaking voice _____			
Mannerisms _____			
Dress code _____			

	How	Who	Pg
Birth marks and scars			
General health			
Disabilities			

Biographical Details

	How	Who	Pg
Named after			
Looks like			
Acts like			
Siblings			
Birth order			
Birth date			
Ethnic origin			
Citizenship			
Marital status			

	How	Who	Pg
Family background			
Born in			
Lives in			
Economic background			
Current economic status			
Education			
Talents and skills			
Occupation			
Professional activities			
Social activities			
Hobbies			
Sports			

	How	Who	Pg
Religious preferences _____			
_____			
Political preferences _____			
_____			

Emotional/Psychological Makeup

	How	Who	Pg
Ambition level _____			
_____			
Moral code _____			
_____			
Habits—good and bad _____			
_____			
Addicted to _____			
_____			
Fears _____			
_____			
Values _____			
_____			
Is impressed by _____			
_____			
Secret dreams _____			
_____			
Public dreams _____			
_____			
Biggest problem _____			
_____			

	How	Who	Pg
Pet peeves			
Likes			
Dislikes			
Biases/prejudices			
Wants most			
Strengths			
Weaknesses			
Other			

EIGHT

SCENES

~~~~~~

We die. That may be the meaning of life. But we do language. That may be the measure of our lives.

—Toni Morrison (author of *Paradise*),
Time magazine, 1996

Two uses of the term *scene* were introduced in chapter 2. The first, book scene, is a subunit of a chapter. Book scenes are identifiable by the blank lines, called scene breaks, that separate them. The second, story scene, is a unit of action in your story taking place over a finite period of time in a specific setting.

In the bestselling *Techniques of the Selling Writer*, Dwight Swain identifies two phases of the story scene, which I term the action phase and the reaction phase. The action phase is a single action or a series of related actions taking place over a finite period of time in a specific setting. The reaction phase of the story scene is the unit of transition that links two action phases. Stories are built from action-reaction sequences. In this chapter, we're going to place Swain's basic building blocks, the action and reaction phases, on our landscape of story scene and book scene.

THE ACTION PHASE

The action phase is composed of three components: goal, conflict, and disaster. In a story scene, at least one character must have a goal. Many times multiple characters in a story scene have a goal and the goals are in conflict with one another, meaning that for one character to achieve her goal another character must not achieve hers. The goal is simply what the character wants. Your character is perhaps after something (information, money, advice) or maybe wants to get rid of something (a burden, information, money, evidence).

Conflict provides the opposition to the character's attainment of her goal. This opposition could take the form of an internal force (fear or love) or an external force (another character or a natural disaster). When the goal and the conflict meet, "disaster" results. Disaster in this sense would be the result of a character achieving her goal or a character being denied her goal. The key is that the disaster provides a new or unexpected development in your story. The character may achieve her goal and get what she wanted only to find that what she wanted is not what she thought it would be.

Suppose a policeman questions a suspect with the goal of getting the name of the person who shot the mayor. The opposition to the goal is the suspect's refusal to divulge any information. The disaster is when the suspect provides proof that the police chief, the policeman's mentor and good friend, hired the suspect to kill the mayor. The policeman achieved his goal and obtained the information he wanted, but it's not the information he expected and now he faces the bigger problem of deciding what to do with the information. This disaster serves as a hook to keep the reader reading. It is a new or unexpected development that keeps the story interesting.

Similarly the disaster could result from the character not

attaining her goal. Suppose a wife goes to her estranged husband's apartment with the goal of reconciling with him. He provides opposition when he meets her at the door and tells her the relationship is over. After they argue in the doorway, she pushes her way into the apartment only to encounter disaster—her best friend seated on the couch with a drink in her hand. Not exactly what the character, or the reader, expected.

THE REACTION PHASE

The reaction phase is also composed of three components: response, dilemma, and decision. Response is the reaction to the disaster that occurred in the action phase. Dilemma is the new question or situation facing the character as a result of the disaster. Decision is the character's answer to her new situation. The decision in the reaction phase leads to the goal in the action phase of the next story scene.

Recall the policeman who's just learned that his friend, the police chief, hired the hit man who killed the mayor. There are a multitude of possible responses to his recently acquired knowledge. Suppose the policeman resists the truth as long as he can, but finally has to admit that the chief is guilty. Not able to handle it, he goes out and gets drunk. When he wakes up the next morning, his first thought is what he should do with the information. He decides to confront the chief.

The response component of this reaction phase is the policeman's initial disbelief and subsequent drinking binge. The dilemma is his realization that he has to do something with his new information. His decision is to confront the chief. The action phase of the next story scene could begin with the policeman confronting the chief with the goal of hearing some explanation of how the evidence was doctored to make the chief look guilty. The opposition could be the chief's guilt. The subsequent disaster could be the chief asking the policeman to get rid of the evidence.

Recall the woman who finds her estranged husband with her best friend. Her reaction could be a violent rage that launches her into a cat fight with her best friend or a quiet rage that sends her running out of the apartment. Her dilemma could be how to go on with her life now that her husband has gone or it could be how to win him back from her no-good best friend. Her decision could be to file for divorce or visit a counselor. If she decides to file for divorce, the next story scene could start with her contacting an attorney with the goal of getting a divorce. If she decides to fight for her husband, her next move could be a visit to a bar on the wrong side of town with the goal of hiring a hit man to kill her friend.

Action-Reaction Sequence Caveats

As with most rules in writing, there is a caveat to the action-reaction method of creating story scenes: Not all of the six components of the action and reaction phases of each story scene have to be written explicitly. Most times one or more of the six components will be implicit. For example, the dilemma and decision may not be explicitly stated in the story but the reader can easily infer it. Consider the example of the woman who found her best friend with her husband. The reaction phase (the rage the woman feels upon seeing her best friend seated in her husband's apartment) could be omitted and the writer could move directly to the scene at the seedy bar with the woman looking for a hit man. The reader can infer from this new story scene that the woman wants to get rid of the competition for her husband's affection. Of course, the writer has to decide which presentation is more effective— including the reaction phase or skipping it and moving directly to the bar.

Likewise, the action phase of the story scene in which the policeman confronts his chief with evidence that he (the chief) hired the hit man to kill the mayor doesn't have to include a long serious conversation between the two men. The policeman could throw the papers on the chief's desk; the chief picks them up and reads them; and then he looks into the policeman's eyes. The policeman looks back and then turns on his heels and leaves the room without the evidence. The goal, conflict, and disaster are presented in that simple exchange.

BUILDING STORY SCENES

Logical Presentation

This discussion of the action-reaction sequence was not presented so that you could dissect each of your story scenes and make sure that you've included each of the six components of the sequence. I explained this sequence to give you a good way to approach story telling. Earlier in this book we introduced set pieces, or key story scenes, around which you should build your story. The other story scenes in your book should flow into or out of your set pieces. The action-reaction sequence clarifies this relationship between story scenes.

How does one story scene flow out of or into another story scene? Simply put, the action of one story scene must have a reaction that leads to the next story scene. Note that I used the terms *action* and *reaction*, not *action phase* and *reaction phase*. I make this distinction because I don't want you to think in terms of components; I want you to think in terms of purpose.

When you're plotting your book and later when you're writing it, you should ask yourself two questions about every story scene: What happened prior to this scene that makes what happens here logical and believable? What might logically happen next as a result of what happened in this scene?

Answering these two questions will help you to make sure that you are building a story that has a logical flow of events.

Remember that each of your story scenes does not have to include all six components of the action-reaction sequence explicitly. Your goal is not to make sure that all the components are written explicitly on the page. Your goal is to make sure that your story flows logically from one story scene to the next.

Physical Presentation

The action-reaction phases for a story scene can appear in a single book scene, or they can continue across multiple book scenes. You can even have more than one action-reaction phase in a book scene. Let's look at some examples:

Book scene 1: Action and reaction phases of story scene 1

Book scene 2: Action phase of story scene 2

Book scene 3: reaction phase of story scene 2 and action phase of story scene 3

Book scene 4: reaction phase of story scene 3

As you can see, book scene 1 contains an entire sequence, while book scenes 2 and 4 contain only one of the phases. Book scene 3 has both phases, but they belong to different story scenes. These four examples illustrate that the writer has discretion in how she packages her story.

Let's look at an example using the first three chapters of the developing plot outline for the novella *The Gift of Love*.

EXAMPLE 12
Action-Reaction Sequence (*The Gift of Love*)

Recall that this story is a novella of about 25,000 words. Brief synopsis: Jackie, the heroine, feels responsible for the death of Kenneth's wife. When she falls in love with him, her guilt forces her to take a new job and leave town. Kenneth, the hero, was secretly in love with her. After she has been gone for a year, he decides to go to her and tell her his feelings.

I have annotated the plot outline for this story with a couple of sentences after each book scene describing the phases of the action-reaction sequence included therein. Remember that the presence of a phase doesn't mean that it's explicitly written into the scene.

Recall that the Roman numerals identify the chapters, and the letters identify the book scenes within the chapter.

I. Kenneth arrives in Trinidad

    A. Kenneth at Jackie's residence; she's not there. Kenneth's POV. Sunday afternoon in Trinidad.
Book scene A will contain the reaction phase of a story scene that occurs before the book starts (story scene 0), and the action and reaction phases of story scene 1. The reaction phase of story scene 0 is included to give the reader a perspective of how Kenneth has fared since he's been separated from Jackie.

    B. Jackie with her friends on Tobago. Jackie's POV. Sunday afternoon in Tobago at the home of Jackie's friends.
Book scene B will contain the reaction phase of a story scene that occurs before the book starts (story scene 0). This scene is included to give the reader a perspective of how Jackie has fared since she's been away from Kenneth and his family.

C. Kenneth finds Jackie on Tobago. Jackie's POV. Sunday evening at the home of Jackie's friends. [*the meet, plot point 1*]
Book scene C will contain the action-reaction phases of story scene 2.

II.   Jackie and Kenneth with Jackie's friends—day 1

A. Jackie takes Kenneth on a tour of the island. Kenneth's POV. Monday morning at a tourist spot on Tobago.
Book scene A will contain the action phase of story scene 3.

B. Kenneth tells Jackie's friends about their friendship. Jackie's POV. Monday midday at a non-tourist restaurant on Tobago.
Book scene B will contain the reaction phase of story scene 3 and the action-reaction phases of story scene 4.

C. Later that night, Kenneth tells Jackie how much she helped him deal with his wife's death. Monday night on the beach near the home of Jackie's friends. [*emotional intimacy, plot point 2*]
Book scene C continues the reaction phase of story scene 4, and includes the action-reaction phases of story scene 5.

III. Janet and Kenneth alone—day 3

A. Kenneth's profession of love. Wednesday midday at Jackie's favorite spot on Tobago. Jackie's POV. [*emotional commitment, plot point 3*]
Book scene A will contain the action phase of story scene 6.

B. Kenneth's confusion. Wednesday midday at Jackie's favorite spot on Tobago. Kenneth's POV.
Book scene B will contain the reaction phase of story scene 6.

C. Jackie's despair. Jackie's POV. Wednesday night at her friends' home.
Book scene C continues the reaction phase of story scene 6.

Discussion

This annotated plot outline shows some ways that you can use the action-reaction sequence to build your story. You should make note of the following observations about the example presented:

1. The first book scene contains the reaction phase for a story scene that's not in the book. Yes, this is nontraditional, but it is a technique that you can use. I plan to incorporate the reaction phase of story scene 0 into the action-reaction phases of story scene 1. I can do this by giving the reader access to Kenneth's thoughts. For example, as Kenneth is preparing to knock on the door of Jackie's home in Trinidad, I may have him think about how stupid he was to let her get away in the first place.

2. You'll notice that the second book scene also includes a reaction phase for story scene 0. I chose to include the reaction phase for story scene 0 in two book scenes because I wanted to show reactions for both Jackie and Kenneth in their individual POVs. The reaction phase in book scene A is in Kenneth's POV, while the one in

book scene B is in Jackie's POV. I use this technique often, as you can see in the outline.

3. Note also that each book scene that contains a plot point–set piece combination also contains an action phase. This occurrence should not be surprising since significant story events are placed at the plot points, and the significant event occurs in the action phase of the story scene.

4. Every story scene presented in the first three chapters, with the exception of story scene 0, has both an action phase and a reaction phase. The presence of the phases in the plot outline does not mean that they will be written explicitly in the story; it does mean that the reader will be able to infer them if they are not written explicitly.

PLOT AND THE ACTION-REACTION PHASES

Up to this point in our discussion of the action-reaction phases, we have considered the development of a single plot line that moves from story scene to story scene, from action phase to reaction phase to action phase to reaction phase, either explicitly or implicitly. We have not considered the impact of supporting plots on the action-reaction sequence.

Generally speaking, there should be an action-reaction thread for the main plot and for each supporting plot. These threads should be woven together in your story. Soap operas provide a good example of how this weaving is done. For example, the CBS soap *The Young and the Restless* may open with a scene of Neil and Dru arguing in their apartment. When the argument reaches a high point, the story may switch to the office of Neil's boss, Victor, who's engaged in a heated argument with his nemesis, Jack. After a commercial break, the show may return to Neil and Dru, or to Victor and Jack, or to a different scene. At some point, though, the show has to return to Neil and Dru so that their story line (or plot) can advance. Likewise, it has to return to Victor and Jack so that their story line (or plot) can advance.

You handle plots and supporting plots in your story much the same way. You build your story by weaving together the story scenes for the main plots and supporting plots.

Let's look at an example using the first three chapters of the developing plot outline for the long mainstream suspense story *To Kill For*.

EXAMPLE 13
Action-Reaction Sequence (*To Kill For*)

Recall that this story is a long suspense novel of about 100,000 words. Brief synopsis: Jackie kills Kenneth's wife, Mary, because she wants Kenneth for herself. Roy, Jackie's ex-husband, thinks his wife is unstable and believes she's capable of murder. When he learns she killed Mary, he protects her because he doesn't want to see her institutionalized. Kenneth is involved in some illegal activity and he thinks his business associates are responsible for his wife's death. He romances Jackie, hoping that she'll give him the money he needs to get his business associates off his back.

This story has a main plot and three supporting plots: Jackie's murder story line (denoted plot A in the outline), Jackie and Kenneth's romantic relationship (plot B), Kenneth's illegal business dealings (plot C), Roy's slow realization that Jackie is seriously disturbed and his attempts to keep Jackie from being institutionalized (plot D).

The Plot Mapping Table below shows the planned placement of story scenes for each of the four plot threads. As the table shows, the thread for plot A goes from 1a to 2a to 3c, and is included in story scenes 1, 4, and 9 respectively; the thread for plot B goes from 1a to 2c and is included in story scenes 1 and 6; the thread for plot C goes from 1c to 3a and includes story scenes 3 and 7; and the thread for plot D goes from 1a to 1b to 2b to 3b and is included in story scenes 1, 2, 5, and 8. The letters AR, which appear after the story scene number, indicate if the Action, Reaction, or both phase of the story scene affects the designated plot. Remember that the presence of a phase doesn't mean that all components of that phase are written explicitly.

STORY SCENE—BOOK SCENE— PLOT MAPPING TABLE

Book Scene	Description	Plot A	Plot B	Plot C	Plot D
1a	Plot point 1—Set piece: The Opening. Jackie and Roy arrive at Mary and Kenneth's for dinner. Jackie still wants Kenneth. Roy realizes he and Kenneth are look-a-likes. Roy's POV for first half; Jackie's POV for remaining.	1:AR	1:AR		1:R
1b	Roy confronts Jackie about his resemblance to Kenneth and begins to worry about her mental state. Roy's POV.				2:AR
1c	Kenneth meets with the associates involved in his illegal business dealings. Kenneth desperate. Kenneth's POV.			3:AR	
2a	Jackie gets friendly with Mary so that she can learn about the state of her marriage to Kenneth. Jackie's POV.	4:AR			

Book Scene	Description	Plot A	Plot B	Plot C	Plot D
2b	Roy visits a doctor to get some advice about Jackie's actions and what they say about her mental health. He thinks about his mother who committed suicide while institutionalized. Roy's POV.				5:AR
2c	Jackie and Kenneth—the flirtation begins. Jackie wants a relationship. Kenneth needs money. Kenneth's POV.		6:AR		
3a	Mary and Kenneth argue about comments his mother has made about his business dealings. Kenneth's POV.			7:AR	
3b	Jackie and Rod argue about her obsession with Kenneth. Rod wants her to get help before it's too late. Rod's POV.				8:AR
3c	Plot point 2—Set piece: First major story turn (around pages 45–50). Mary's tragic car accident. Jackie's POV.	9:AR			

Discussion

The annotated outline presented in the Plot Mapping Table shows some ways that you can use the action-reaction sequence to build a story that has a main plot and one or more supporting plots. You should make note of the following observations about the example presented:

1. A single story scene can support more than one plot. For example, 1a supports both the main plot A, and the

supporting plots B and D. In the reaction phase Roy realizes that he looks like Kenneth and begins to question his wife's stability. This reaction phase, which is in Roy's POV, sets up plot D, which continues in 1b. The portion of 1a that is in Jackie's POV sets up plot B, which continues in 2c (Jackie flirting with Kenneth).

2. The movements for the individual plots are not consecutive. Instead, the four plots are interwoven. The movement of plot A is from 1a (the dinner) to 2a (Mary and Jackie bonding) to 3c (Mary's murder). The movement of plot C is from 1c (Kenneth meeting with his business partners) to 3a (Kenneth and Mary arguing). The movement of plot D is from 1b (Roy confronting Jackie about her obsession with Kenneth) to 2b (Roy seeking outside advice about his wife's mental condition) to 3b (Roy arguing with Jackie about her feelings for Kenneth). The movement for plot B is from 1a (the dinner) to 2c (Jackie flirting with Kenneth).

3. Story scene 1 in 1a and story scene 3 in 1c do not have lead-in, or setup, scenes. Story scene 1 can't have a lead-in since it's the first chapter in the book. It is not unusual for an early scene, like 1c, to lack a lead-in scene. Again, at this early point in the book, you are establishing your conflict. If this scene appeared later in the book without a lead-in scene, I would caution you to verify that the scene is logically placed.

Dangers of Not Using the Action-Reaction Sequence

A common problem for new writers is the absence of what many refer to as flow. Many times their stories aren't told with any sense of connectivity or orderliness. Something will happen, something else will happen, then yet another thing happens, but there is no clear connection between the events. Sometimes the story is not even told in chronological order. If you follow the action-reaction sequence to construct your story scenes and the overarching story, you will be forced to tell your story with a sense of order. Events in chapter 2 will occur as a result of what happened in chapter 1. You'll be writing your story with an eye on keeping the reader interested.

Books that fail to employ the action-reaction sequence generally suffer from a second malady: dull characters with no appeal to the reader. Readers find it difficult to care about characters when nothing of consequence happens to them. If you use the action-reaction sequence to build your story scenes, you will not write boring characters. Instead, you will write characters who move through the story with purpose. Your characters will face challenges as they encounter opposition to their goals. They will have successes and failures. Many times, these failures will lead them to regroup before they continue on their purposeful way. As the readers experience the characters' lives with them, they will get to know them and they will grow to care about them.

EXERCISE 18

18.1. Take your favorite book and identify three action-reaction sequences. Label the components. Remember that all six components don't have to be written explicitly.

18.1.1. Which character is the POV character?

18.1.2. What is this character's goal?

18.1.3. What's keeping the character from attaining the goal?

18.1.4. What do we learn about the POV character in the scene?

18.1.5. What do we learn about the other characters?

18.1.6. What question is left to the reader at the end of the passage?

18.2. In chapters 3 and 4, you began developing a plot outline for your story. Your outline included chapter designations and brief descriptions of the scenes that you planned to include in each chapter. Update your plot outline to reflect the book scenes that you're going to include in each of the first three chapters. For each book scene, indicate the POV character, the place, and the time. If you are unable to outline the three chapters, revisit your characters and do more research. Remember that building the plot outline is a task you'll return to time and again as the pieces of your story take shape.

NINE

CHAPTERS

~~~~~~

As a young girl curled up on the couch reading Romeo and Juliet, *I was convinced the voices rising from the page were mine—my mind's whisperings, the unformed hopes and desperate yearnings of an adolescent soul. Years later I read that devastating opening chapter of James Baldwin's* Another Country *and discovered a different voice—the voice of a Black man driven by society's intolerance and desperate measures. The tune was the same; only the arrangement was different. The eloquence of Romeo and Juliet's love ultimately shamed their detractors; Baldwin's wrenching description of Rufus's suicide is bearable only because it is a searing indictment of hate in any society.*

—Rita Dove
(author of *On the Bus with Rosa Parks*),
Essence magazine, 1995

Chapters, though they seem to be very important, are really artificial constructs that make a book easier to read. They serve as containers for one or more book scenes. Chapters are for the reader. They provide an easily identifiable stopping place in the story so that if the reader has to put the book down she can easily pick up later where she left off. You could write your story as a single chapter but your reader would find it difficult to read. Bottom line: you choose chapters, they don't choose you.

I am often asked how many pages a chapter should have, how many scenes. The answer to both questions is as many as you want. Generally, I plot my books with the goal of three book scenes to a chapter and shoot for fifteen to twenty pages per chapter. I don't know how or why I adopted that method, but it seems to work for me. Of course, I'll sometimes have chapters with more than three book scenes and more than twenty pages. Other times I'll have chapters with fewer than three book scenes and fewer than fifteen pages.

Ultimately, a chapter's length isn't anywhere near as important as how effective it is. I like to end each chapter with either the disaster component, the response component, the dilemma component, or the decision component of the story scene. These components usually have an element of surprise or change in them, elements that will keep the reader turning pages. These elements are called hooks. You want to hook the reader and keep her reading.

In addition to ending with a hook, a chapter should also begin with a hook. Choosing an effective ending to a chapter sets you up for an effective beginning to the next chapter. An effective opening starts in the middle of action already underway.

Suppose your story is about a man who robs a bank because he's lost his job and thinks that his wife will leave him when he runs out of money. If the man's problems start when he marries his wife then don't start your story when the man is born and tell his entire life story up to the point that he gets married. You might want to start with his marriage, or the day he finds out that his wife loves money more than she loves him, or the day he loses his job, or the day he decides to pull the bank heist, or the day of the bank heist. The closer to the big event you start your story, the more powerful the opening. By starting your story with the wedding you'll have a very different book with a different emphasis from what you'll have if you begin the action on the day of the bank heist. Choose the opening that's most effective for the story you want to tell, the opening that will pull your reader into that story. Resist the temptation to start with background information. Throw the reader into the story and feed her background information in small doses as you tell your story.

Let's look at the first passage of three effective first chapters.

You see, I growed up in a place called Annington County, Mississippi.

In my day, colored folk up and died whenever white folk got a notion for us to. Mostly our men, but sometimes women and children. You look up one day and they gone, like a speck of dirt just blowing on the breeze. Sometimes with grown-ups, you almost had to remember if they was ever there in the first place, because you couldn't tell who was who by the graves. But with children, there was never no wondering. People always left rocks behind, sticks, X's, half-pushed in the ground. It was parents' way of burying parts of themselves with their babies. What remained, they numbed, just to get by

Dawn Turner Trice, *Only Twice I Wished for Heaven*
(Crown Publishing, 1996)

The preceding passage was taken from a book written in first-person POV. The distinctive voice of the narrator opens the story and the reader is thrown into the middle of the narrator's discourse on death and black folks and white folks in Mississippi. The questions arise immediately: What is this narrator talking about? Who died and what did white folks have to do with it? The reader gets the sinking feeling that a child is dead, and she wants to read further, hoping against hope that she's wrong and a child isn't dead. Trice has created a powerful opening here.

Chicago
May 1884

Under the cover of the darkness, Katherine Love stood with her back pressed closely against the outside wall of the warehouse, hoping she couldn't be seen. The night watchman was on the far side of the yard, and she was waiting for him to pass. She could see him walking and swinging his lantern in and out of the shadows. He was whistling cheerily as he checked a few doors to make sure they hadn't been tampered with, but he gave no more than a cursory look to most of the sheds and buildings along the route.

This was the third night Katherine had come here hoping to rendezvous with a man hired to assist her in her plan, but for reasons unknown, he'd never shown. She hoped this third night would be the charm.

Beverly Jenkins, *Topaz* (Avon Books, 1997)

This passage, taken from a book written in limited third-person POV, starts in the middle of the action. Katherine Love is hiding out to meet some mystery man who's going to help her with some problem. The reader has nothing but questions. What is Katherine's problem? Why is she meeting the man at night? Why is she hiding? Will she get caught? These questions intrigue the reader and encourage her to keep reading for the answers.

Notice that this chapter starts with a date and place, which is common for novels set in the past or the future. The date and place readily situate the reader in the story.

"Come get me."
When Betty picked up the receiver of the cream-colored wall phone, the voice on the other end was already speaking. It sounded as if it came from the grave.
"Come get me. Come . . . get . . . me. Come . . . get . . .

me," the voice kept repeating slowly, deliberately, as if each word carried some special meaning.

Betty turned her head away from the phone and massaged her temples.

"Damn," she said to her sister Emily, who was sitting at the rec room bar looking at herself in the mirror through rows of glasses and through a stack of her father's science fiction magazines. Emily fiddled with her thick black shiny bangs awhile and finally pulled them back behind her ears with the rest of her hair, blow-dried straight and even nearly down to her shoulders. "We ain't even had Murdear's funeral yet and the Lovejoy family is already falling apart. It's Annie Ruth."

Tina McElroy Ansa, *Ugly Ways* (Harcourt Brace, 1993)

Ansa's book, also written in limited third-person POV, opens with dialogue. The reader is again thrown into the middle of the action, and introduced to a set of questions. The family is getting ready for a funeral and Annie Ruth is in trouble. The reader is not sure yet exactly what kind of trouble, but she'll probably read on to find out.

EXERCISE 19

Visit the fiction section of your local library or bookstore and find three books that you haven't read by authors that you don't usually read. Read the first three chapters of each book and answer the following questions:

19.1. How does each chapter start: with dialogue, interior monologue, showing, telling?

19.2. Does each chapter begin and end with a hook?

19.3. How many book scenes are in each chapter?

19.4. How many pages are in each book scene? in each chapter?

19.5. Do you see any pattern in your answers to questions 19.1—19.4? If so, what is it?

19.6. Which book has the most compelling opening? What makes the opening compelling?

19.7. Which book would you buy? Why?

TEN

TO WRITE IS TO REVISE

There is an illusion that black writers are being published in great numbers. What we have to do is distinguish between authors and writers. A lot of people are under the impression that every author is a writer; it's not necessarily so.

—Marie Brown (literary agent),
Black Enterprise magazine,
1997

When you finish that last chapter and type THE END, your book is finished and you're ready to send it to a publisher or an agent. Right? Wrong. After you finish the first draft, you move into the revision phase. Revision is the author reviewing, correcting, and, in many cases, rewriting her work to make the story stronger, more compelling. The revision process is unique for each author and each author's process is refined with each book.

Different writers do their editing at different times. Some writers revise as they write. After they type THE END, they do a final read-through of their manuscript, make some minor corrections, and then they're done. Those writers belong to a fortunate minority. Most writers write with the knowledge that they're going to do two, three, or (most times), many more drafts of their manuscript to get it just right. I'm in that latter group. I write the cleanest first draft that I can write, but I know that I'll have to go back after the draft is finished and make revisions. In this chapter, we'll discuss three levels of revisions. First-level revisions are the revisions authors make while writing the first draft; second-level revisions are revisions made after the first draft is complete; third-level revisions are revisions done after the author has put some distance between herself and her manuscript.

FIRST-LEVEL REVISIONS

First-level revisions are a major challenge for many writers because revising can be a deterrent to finishing the story. In the writer's determination to perfect each chapter, scene, sentence, and word, he can become mired in the revision process, unable to complete the first draft. Therefore, the writer has to develop some balance between writing and revising in order to complete the all-important first draft. Using the 1-3-100 method of writing and revising the first draft has proved effective for me.

The 1-3-100 method has three steps:

Step 1. Revise each chapter after it is written (1).

Step 2. Revise after every third chapter is written (3).

Step 3. Revise after every 100 pages are written (100).

In the 1-3-100 method, the writer writes the first chapter, reads it, revises it, and then moves on to the second chapter. He repeats this process for chapters two and three. After chapter 3 is revised, the author reads the first three chapters as a whole, revises them, and moves on to chapter 4.

The author continues this process of revising after each chapter and revising again after every third chapter until he reaches the chapter that includes page 100. After that chapter is written and revised, the author reads all the chapters, from chapter 1 through the chapter that includes page 100. He revises those chapters and moves on to the next one. He continues to write and revise using the 1-3-100 method until the first draft of his book is complete.

SECOND-LEVEL REVISIONS

Once the first draft is finished, second-level revisions begin. While first-level revisions are applied to sections of your book, second-level revisions are applied to the entire book. The first step in second-level revisions is to read the manuscript from beginning to end, preferably in one, uninterrupted reading session. The goal of this read-through is for you to get an overview of your book. As you read, you should jot down the concerns and questions that arise. Notes can range from circling a misspelled word and correcting punctuation, to questioning the accuracy of details. Notes that I've made include: "sounds funny," "boring," "why is she saying this?" "didn't she say the opposite somewhere earlier in the story?" "make sure her eyes are still the same color," "how old is she here?" and "does this make sense?"

Sometimes you will know immediately what changes need to be made and you should note those changes. Other times, you'll identify a problem but you won't know immediately how to fix it. Just make a note and keep reading. Again, the goal at this point is to read through the entire book, not to fix every problem you find on the spot.

Once you complete the read-through, go back to the beginning of the manuscript and address the notes you made. Your goal is to fix the problems you uncovered in your read-through. This step can take anywhere from a few days to a few weeks, depending on the amount of time you write each day and the severity of the problems you find.

The next phase of second-level revisions is another read-through of the manuscript. The goal of this read-through is to construct a book scene summary table for your manuscript. An easy way to construct the summary table is to use your word processor's table function to create a table with the number of rows equal to the number of chapters in your book and the number of columns equal to the maximum number of book scenes you have in a chapter. Each cell represents a specific scene in a specific chapter. After the table is constructed, you record the location, date, day, and time of each scene, the characters involved (identifying the POV character), and the key event in the scene.

The completed summary table is a powerful tool for revising. You can use it to verify key components of your story, including:

1. *Timeline.* Since you've recorded dates, days, and times in the table, you can verify that events in your story happen over a reasonable time period. Sometimes when I'm writing I lose track of days. For example, I may have a character leaving on a three-day business trip on Monday and returning home on Sunday. The summary table reveals this error, leaving me with the choice of changing the trip to a seven-day trip, changing the return day to Thursday, or sending the character on a four-day vacation before she returns home.

2. *Holidays, birthdays, anniversaries.* The summary table will remind you to consider days, dates, holidays, birthdays, and anniversaries. For example, if your book starts in September of one year and ends in March of the next year, you should have some reference to the holidays that occur during that period unless your characters have a reason for ignoring them. If the book extends beyond a year, somebody needs to have a birthday—or at least mention a birthday—or there should be a reason why there is no mention.

3. *Character locations*. The summary table also helps you verify that all your characters are in the right place at the right time. I once had a hero go to dinner with the heroine in their hometown after the hero had left town on a business trip. He would have had to be some kind of hero to accomplish that! The summary table makes this type of blunder obvious.

4. *Plot*. The summary table allows you to check the plot and pacing of your story. You can easily locate your plot points and determine if they're effectively placed. When writing a 400-page book, I'll do spot checks at the end of chapter 3 and around pages 100, 200, 300, and 375, to make sure significant events are unfolding at those points.

5. *POV*. The summary table also allows you to check which POVs are used most frequently. If you're writing a limited third-person POV story, you want to make sure that a large majority, if not all, of your scenes use the POV of a leading character.

After checking the summary table for these types of inconsistencies, you are ready to make the changes to the manuscript and print a clean copy for yet another read-through. If you find it difficult to read through the manuscript this time, you're not alone. Repeatedly reading the manuscript is the toughest part of revision for most writers. Before the revision process is complete, don't be surprised if you feel as though you never want to read the story again.

Second-level revisions can continue through five or more drafts of your manuscript. It's a process of reading your manuscript, revising it, printing it, and reading it again. Second-level revisions end when you reach a point of diminishing returns, the point at which you're making insignificant changes to your manuscript.

EXAMPLE 14
Book Scene Summary Table

Consider the first three rows from the book scene summary table example I developed for one of my books:

Chapter 1 Day 1. Friday evening. Hampton's patio. Ms. Hampton, Marlena, Reginald McCoy, Frank Thomas. POV: Marlena	Patio to dining room. Winston, McCoy, Marlena. They watch each other. POV: Winston	Dining room to library. Marlena, Winston, Yolanda. Winston asks for her help on *the way home* and she agrees. POV: Marlena	Saturday a.m. Hotel lobby then Marlena's room and shower. Marlena, Billy, bellhop. She misses him, but gets his note. He calls and schedules the meeting. POV: Marlena	
Chapter 2 Marlena's hotel room. Marlena calls Cheryl. Is invited to come over. POV: Marlena	Cheryl's house—living room and kitchen. Cheryl, Marlena, Patrice. The women catch up. POV: Marlena	Day 2. Saturday morning. Winston's mother's house—dining room. Winston, his mother, Martha. His mother challenges him about Marlena. POV: Winston	Saturday a.m. Hotel lobby. Winston, Billy. He goes to see her on the pretext of scheduling a meeting. She's not home. UPDATE: Winston's POV, use it to show more about him.	
Chapter 3 Saturday morning. The projects. Cheryl and Marlena go visiting. They visit with older lady who knew Marlena's mom. They visit Nancy. POV: Marlena	Saturday afternoon. Winston sees Marlena at park. Billy jokes with Winston about Marlena. POV: Winston	Saturday afternoon. Ball field. Yolanda comes over to talk to Marlena, snubs Nancy and Cheryl. POV: Marlena	UPDATE: Saturday afternoon. After ball game. Cheryl's car, leaving Dustown going to Cheryl's house.	Cheryl's yard and front porch. Cheryl, Marlena, Raymond, Patrice. They talk about their feelings for their exes. POV: Marlena

This sample summary table shows three rows indicating the first three chapters of the book. It has five columns, indicating that it can support as many as five book scenes per chapter. Only one chapter in this sample table, chapter 2, has five scenes. The table shows that these first three chapters cover two days of the story. Day one, Friday, starts in the first scene of chapter 1 and day two, Saturday, starts in the third scene of chapter 2.

The UPDATE tag in scene 4 of chapters 2 and 3 indicate a change I made to that scene based on my review of the summary table. In chapter 2, scene 4, I inserted a scene in Winston's POV (the leading male character) so that I could give more of his inner thoughts early in the story. In these three chapters, Marlena (the leading female character) has eight POV scenes to Winston's four.

In chapter 3, scene 4, instead of starting the book scene in Cheryl's yard, I decided to start it at the ball park and continue it through to Cheryl's yard. Notice that even though the setting changed from the ball park to Cheryl's yard, the book scene didn't. I didn't include a scene break because the event was a continuous action (the car ride from the park to Cheryl's house) in a single POV. The same is true in chapter 3, scene 1, where Cheryl and Marlena visit the homes of two different friends in the same book scene. In this case, I didn't include a scene break because I treated the setting as the housing projects in their old neighborhood, not the individual homes.

THIRD-LEVEL REVISIONS

Third-level revisions begin after the writer has taken a break from the work in progress, usually a week or more. I've found this distance to be one of the most important parts of the revision process. After you read through your manuscript a few times, you begin to read *what you meant to write* instead of *what you actually wrote*. You are too close to your work to have any objectivity about it. Taking a week—more time if you have it—away from your manuscript will give you the needed distance and objectivity. When you come back to the manuscript, you'll be able to read it with fresh eyes—eyes that see *what you wrote* instead of *what you meant to write*.

After the distancing period is over, you should return again to the process of reading, revising, printing, and rereading the manuscript until you are satisfied you have told the story to the best of your ability. This point of satisfaction is not easily identifiable because there is always one more tweak that can be made, just one more small change. Most writers struggle with letting go of a manuscript, but they get better at it with each book. After nine books, I'm finding the point of satis-faction easier to identify though I still struggle with needing to do just one more read-through to get the story right.

New writers often find it especially difficult to let go of their manuscript. This difficulty is usually tied to their skill as writ-ers. Because new writers develop skills in huge leaps, they often find that the later parts of their books reflect a much higher level of writing skill than do the beginning parts. Sometimes hard work on the author's part can salvage a book with this imbalance, but many times the author is better served by leav-ing that book and moving on to a new one. I know that it's hard to even think of walking away from a book that you've slaved over and a story that you've come to love, but your time will be better spent working on a new story that you can start fresh with your improved writing skills. There is no payoff in trying to breathe life into a story that will be at best mediocre.

The three-level revision process described above is an ideal process. No one follows it precisely. After you sell your first book and begin writing to contract, external factors begin to play a role in your writing life. With some books, the deadline dictates how much distance you'll be able to give yourself from the manuscript before you have to submit it. You'll have to learn how much time it takes you to write a solid book and build that time (plus time for unexpected events like sickness and car trouble) into your contract schedule. If you haven't sold a book yet, use this time to develop good writing habits. Write often. Write more than one book. You will write three books or more before you get a firm handle on how much time it takes you to write a story. So keep writing. Don't stop.

REVISION CHECKLIST

Revision basically comes down to applying the rules of good writing to your completed draft. In this sense, revision is the process of making sure that you did what you were supposed to do when you were writing the book. It can be likened to the quality control function in a manufacturing facility. Inspection allows manufacturers to see how well they met their quality goals and to fix or tweak areas where they missed the mark. The same applies to your story. You must follow the rules of good writing as you're writing your story; then you use the revision process to shore up those areas where you missed the mark.

The Revision Checklist guides you through a quality check of your manuscript. It is divided into eight categories—plot, characters, research, point of view, dialogue, showing and telling, scenes, and chapters—representing the major topic areas covered in this book. Within each area the Revision Checklist provides a series of questions that you should apply to your manuscript when doing first-, second- and third-level revisions.

Plot

1. Is the story built around an identifiable conflict?

2. Have plot points and set pieces been employed to move the story along at a pace that keeps the reader reading, or does the story drag in places?

3. Does the book open with a hook?

4. Does the opening of the book give the reader some clue to the basic story conflict?

Characters

1. Is each character uniquely identifiable?

2. Do the leading characters have goals and conflicts that direct their actions and reactions throughout the story?

3. Are supporting characters and extras used to provide insight into the leading characters, or to move the story forward, or both?

4. Do the characters have sufficient motivation for each of their actions?

5. Do the characters grow and change over the course of the story?

Research

1. Has all factual information been verified?

2. Are settings described with enough detail to provide a real sense of place to the reader?

3. Are character occupations and hobbies presented in a realistic manner?

Point of View

1. How many points of view are used in each book scene? If more than one is used, is there a valid reason for switching viewpoints?

2. If multiple points of view are used, can the reader easily tell whose POV is being used at all times?

Interior Monologue

1. Is interior monologue limited to the point-of-view character?

2. Does interior monologue move the story forward or reveal character or both?

Dialogue

1. Does the dialogue really sound like people are speaking?

2. Does the dialogue read like "talking heads"?

3. Have speaker attributions been used unnecessarily when the reader can easily tell who's speaking?

4. Does dialogue move the story forward or reveal character or both?

5. Does each character have a unique speaking voice that distinguishes him from other characters?

6. Is the dialogue punctuated correctly?

Showing and Telling

1. Have *showing* passages been used to show the reader the important scenes of the story as well as the emotions of the characters?

2. Have *telling* passages been used to move the reader through unimportant information or activity?

3. Have strong, active verbs and specific nouns been used instead of general nouns and passive or weak verbs to paint vivid images for the reader?

Scenes

1. Does the story scene construction follow the action-reaction sequence?

2. Is the time, place, and viewpoint character of each book scene readily identifiable?

3. Does each book scene end with a hook or a question in the reader's mind?

Chapters

1. Are the chapters packaged so that each one starts with a hook and ends with a hook?

2. Does your first chapter start in the middle of some action that is already occurring?

3. Are the chapter openings varied with respect to the use of dialogue, interior monologue, showing, and telling?

Voice

1. Has sensory detail from each of the five senses been used to make passages alive for the reader?

2. Have all unnecessary words and redundant information been cut?

3. Is correct grammar used except in cases where incorrect usage is intended?

EXERCISE 20

20.1. If you have completed the plot outline for the first three chapters of your book, write those chapters using the 1-3-100 method. If you can use the method to write your first three chapters, you can use it to write your entire first draft. If you haven't completed the plot outline for those chapters, take some time now to work on it.

20.2. After you finish writing your first three chapters, create a book scene summary table and use it to uncover the revision needs in those chapters. If you can use the summary table to help you uncover revision needs for your first three chapters, you can use it to help you uncover revision needs for your finished manuscript.

20.3. You should keep the Revision Checklist handy as you write. You might even consider posting it someplace over your desk. After you have revised your first three chapters, review the checklist again and decide if you want additional topic areas or additional questions. Customizing this list is essential to making it effective in helping you write and revise your manuscript. For example, if you use the word *really* too frequently, you could add an "Overused Words" topic area and include a question to remind yourself to check your use of *really*.

FINAL WORDS

~~~~~~

Music, chiefly hip-hop, plays an important role in my writing. There is not a day that I do not listen to Black music: jazz, gospel, Motown, Stax, or the blues. I can read a James Baldwin poem and feel a jazz riff. With most of our younger writers under thirty, hip-hop is an obvious influence. Just like in music, a renaissance is going on with young writers of my generation—playwrights, essayists, poets, and novelists. Some people are critical of them because too many of these young writers want to be instant stars. They don't understand that it takes time to achieve any status. You have got to do your homework. There has to be a connection between the young and the older Black male writers. Some of them don't know who Langston Hughes, Sonia Sanchez, or Dudley Randall are. They must realize we owe our elders a lot.

—Arthur Flowers
(author of *Another Good Loving Blues*),
World Wide Web, 1997

My biggest fear when giving writing advice is that someone will actually take it. Not really. I fear that people will treat what I offer as *a* method for writing and revising a manuscript as *the only* method. If you take that position, you will have missed the entire point of this book.

I started this book with a discussion of the writer's voice and I think it appropriate that I end it the same way because your voice is the most valuable resource you bring to the writing process. It's important for you to understand the rules of the writing craft and to know what other writers do, but it's more important that you develop your own way. You must make your writing and your writing process your own.

So I ask that you use this book as a starting point, not as the final word. Try my methods and see if they work for you. Don't be afraid to vary a technique I've presented to make it work better for you.

Finally, I wish you good success in your writing endeavors. Enjoy the process of writing and take pride in your every accomplishment, regardless of how small each may seem.

APPENDIX A

WORSHEETS

GOAL-SETTING WORKSHEET

For writing:

I will write _____ pages each _____ .

OR

I will write for _____ hours each _____ .

I will start on _____ .

For reading craft books:

I will read _____ craft book(s) each _____ .

OR

I will read craft books for _____ hours each _____ .

My first/next craft book will be _____ .

I will start it on _____ .

For reading genre books:

I will read _____ genre book(s) each _____ .

OR

I will read genre books for _____ hours each _____ .

My first/next genre book will be _____ .

I will start it on _____ .

CHARACTER PROFILE WORKSHEET

Copy this worksheet and complete as needed for leading and secondary characters. Space is provided for you to add attributes.

Name _____

Physical Attributes

Sex _____

_____

Age _____

_____

Height _____

_____

Build _____

_____

Eyes _____

_____

Skin _____

_____

Hair _____

_____

Speaking voice _____

_____

Mannerisms _____

_____

Dress code _____

_____

Birth marks and scars _____

General health _____

Disabilities _____

Biographical Details

Named after _____

Looks like _____

Acts like _____

Siblings _____

Birth order _____

Birth date _____

Ethnic origin _____

Citizenship _____

Marital status _____

Family background _____

_____

Born in _____

_____

Lives in _____

_____

Economic background _____

_____

Current economic status _____

_____

Education _____

_____

Talents and skills _____

_____

Occupation _____

_____

Professional activities _____

_____

Social activities _____

_____

Hobbies _____

_____

Sports _____

_____

Religious preferences _____

_____

Political preferences _____

_____

Emotional/Psychological Makeup

Ambition level _____

_____

Moral code _____

_____

Habits—good and bad _____

_____

Addicted to _____

_____

Fears _____

_____

Values _____

_____

Is impressed by _____

_____

Secret dreams _____

_____

Public dreams _____

_____

Biggest problem _____

_____

Pet peeves _____

_____

Likes _____

_____

Dislikes _____

_____

Biases/prejudices _____

_____

Wants most _____

_____

Strengths _____

_____

Weaknesses _____

_____

Other _____

_____

_____

_____

_____

_____

_____

MODIFIED CHARACTER PROFILE WORKSHEET

Book title: _____

Number of pages: _____

Key:

How refers to how the information about the character is presented to the reader: internal monologue (IM), dialogue (D), showing (S), telling (T)

Who refers to the character who reveals the information: self (S), another leading character (LC), supporting character (SC), extra (E)

	How	Who	Pg
Name _____			
_____			
Physical Attributes			
Sex _____			
_____			
Age _____			
_____			
Height _____			
_____			
Build _____			
_____			
Eyes _____			
_____			

	How	Who	Pg
Skin _____			
_____			
Hair _____			
_____			
Speaking voice _____			
_____			
Mannerisms _____			
_____			
Dress code _____			
_____			
Birth marks and scars _____			
_____			
General health _____			
_____			
Disabilities _____			
_____			

Biographical Details

	How	Who	Pg
Named after _____			
_____			
Looks like _____			
_____			
Acts like _____			
_____			
Siblings _____			
_____			

	How	Who	Pg
Birth order			
Birth date			
Ethnic origin			
Citizenship			
Marital status			
Family background			
Born in			
Lives in			
Economic background			
Current economic status			
Education			
Talents and skills			
Occupation			

	How	Who	Pg
Professional activities			
Social activities			
Hobbies			
Sports			
Religious preferences			
Political preferences			

Emotional/Psychological Makeup

	How	Who	Pg
Ambition level			
Moral code			
Habits—good and bad			
Addicted to			
Fears			
Values			

	How	Who	Pg
Is impressed by			
Secret dreams			
Public dreams			
Biggest problem			
Pet peeves			
Likes			
Dislikes			
Biases/prejudices			
Wants most			
Strengths			
Weaknesses			
Other			

REVISION CHECKLIST

Plot

1. Is the story built around an identifiable conflict?
2. Have plot points and set pieces been employed to move the story along at a pace that keeps the reader reading, or does the story drag in places?
3. Does the book open with a hook?
4. Does the opening of the book give the reader some clue to the basic story conflict?

Characters

1. Is each character uniquely identifiable?
2. Do the leading characters have goals and conflicts that direct their actions and reactions throughout the story?
3. Are supporting characters and extras used to provide insight into the leading characters, or to move the story forward, or both?
4. Do the characters have sufficient motivation for each of their actions?
5. Do the characters grow and change over the course of the story?

Research

1. Has all factual information been verified?
2. Are settings described with enough detail to provide a real sense of place to the reader?
3. Are character occupations and hobbies presented in a realistic manner?

Point of View

1. How many points of view are used in each book scene? If more than one is used, is there a valid reason for switching viewpoints?
2. If multiple points of view are used, can the reader easily tell whose POV is being used at all times?

Interior Monologue

1. Is interior monologue limited to the point-of-view character?
2. Does interior monologue move the story forward or reveal character or both?

Dialogue

1. Does the dialogue really sound like people are speaking?
2. Does the dialogue read like "talking heads"?
3. Have speaker attributions been used unnecessarily when the reader can easily tell who's speaking?
4. Does dialogue move the story forward or reveal character or both?
5. Does each character have a unique speaking voice that distinguishes him from other characters?
6. Is the dialogue punctuated correctly?

Showing and Telling

1. Have *showing* passages been used to show the reader the important scenes of the story as well as the emotions of the characters?
2. Have *telling* passages been used to move the reader through unimportant information or activity?
3. Have strong, active verbs and specific nouns been

used instead of general nouns and passive or weak verbs to paint vivid images for the reader?

Scenes

1. Does the story scene construction follow the action-reaction sequence?

2. Is the time, place, and viewpoint character of each book scene readily identifiable?

3. Does each book scene end with a hook or a question in the reader's mind?

Chapters

1. Are the chapters packaged so that each one starts with a hook and ends with a hook?

2. Does your first chapter start in the middle of some action that is already occurring?

3. Are the chapter openings varied with respect to the use of dialogue, interior monologue, showing, and telling?

Voice

1. Has sensory detail from each of the five senses been used to make passages alive for the reader?

2. Have all unnecessary words and redundant information been cut?

3. Is correct grammar used except in cases where incorrect usage is intended?

EXERCISES

~~~~~~

EXERCISE 1

You have to define success for yourself. My only advice is not to let your success be defined by forces beyond your control. The following questions will help you think through success and what it means to you and your writing career.

1.1. What criteria do you use to measure success? Why do you use those criteria?

1.2. List your three favorite authors. Find out when they started writing, the number of books they wrote before they sold their first story, and at least one anecdote about how they overcame adversity in their career. Start with back issues of popular magazines and major newspapers. Your local library has indexes that can help you locate the information you need.

1.3. Review what you've learned about your favorite authors. How successful do you consider them to be?

1.4. What expectations do you have for your writing future? Do you think those expectations are realistic? What are you doing to enhance your chances for success?

EXERCISE 2

2.1. Go to the mall or the park or any place where you can observe people in action. Take a pad and pencil and a friend with you. A writer friend would be good, but any friend will do. Your assignment is to observe and record. Pick a person or a storefront or a sign and spend five minutes writing a description of it. Be sure to use all your senses as you write your description. Write what you see and what you don't see. Write what you feel, both physically and emotionally. Write the sounds you hear and the thoughts you think as you observe. When the five minutes are up, focus on something else. Continue this assignment for at least an hour. When you're done, compare notes with your friend. Talk about the differences and similarities in your observations. When you complete this exercise, you should have some clear examples of how voice determines what you see, how you see it, and how you choose to describe it.

2.2. Your voice influences your reading preferences. The following exercises will demonstrate that influence.

2.2.1. List the last ten novels you've read.

2.2.2. Why did you read these books?

2.2.3. What did you like best about them?

2.2.4. What did you like least about them?

2.2.5. If you could rewrite the stories, what, if anything, would you change in them? Why would you make these changes?

EXERCISE 3

3.1. The following questions will help you begin to identify the hindrances to your writing:

3.1.1. What should you be doing now to move forward with your writing? If you aren't doing these things, make a list of the activities and commitments that prevent you from doing them.

3.1.2. Are your family and friends aware of your need to write? Are they supportive? If they aren't, what can you do to compensate for their lack of support? If they are, how do you show them that you appreciate their support?

3.2 Answer the next two questions to give yourself some insight into steps to take to overcome your hindrances.

3.2.1. What are you willing to give up, or sacrifice, to become a better writer?

3.2.2. Do you belong to a writers support group of some kind, for example, a critique group or a readers group? Your local library or college is a good place to find such groups. If there are no such groups in your area, then you might ask your local librarian to start a list of patrons interested in forming one.

3.3. Complete the Goal-Setting Worksheet on page 188. If the timelines presented on the worksheet don't work for you, modify them to meet your lifestyle and your needs. The key to accomplishing your goals is setting realistic ones. The only thing worse than having no goals is having goals that you have no chance of achieving.

EXERCISE 4

Answer the first two questions below for the books you listed in exercise 2.2.1.

4.1. Is each book plot-driven or character-driven?

4.2. What are each book's external and internal conflicts?

4.3. Is the book you're writing (or starting to write) character-driven or plot-driven?

4.4. What is the external conflict in your story?

4.5. What are the internal conflicts of each of the lead characters in your story?

EXERCISE 5

Answer the following questions for each book you listed in exercise 2.2.1.

5.1. How many book scenes are in the first three chapters of each book?

5.2. Can you identify the first story scene?

EXERCISE 6

6.1. If you're writing a genre story and you have a publisher that you're targeting, write to that publisher and request guidelines.

6.2. Using the first three steps of the plotting-by-genre method, identify the plot points and develop a two- to three-word general description for each of the associated set pieces. It's likely that you won't be able to identify a set piece for each plot point on your first try.

EXERCISE 7

7.1. Following the examples presented in this section, complete the free-writing and outlining exercises for your story.

EXERCISE 8

8.1. Identify the lead characters in a book you've read recently. What makes those characters memorable? Which character is the protagonist? How do you know?

8.2. Identify the supporting characters in the same story. What do you learn about the leading characters from their interaction with the supporting characters? What role do the supporting characters play in advancing the plot?

8.3. Identify the extras in the same story. What do you learn about the leading characters from their interaction with the extras? What role do the extras play in advancing the plot?

8.4. Identify the lead characters and key supporting characters in your story.

EXERCISE 9

9.1. Describe the lead characters you identified in exercise 8 and discuss what makes them distinct and unique characters.

9.2. Describe the supporting characters you identified in exercise 8 and discuss what makes them distinct and unique characters.

9.3 Describe the leading and supporting characters in your story and discuss what makes them distinct or unique. Do not be dismayed if you have trouble doing so.

EXERCISE 10

10.1. List some of the character types commonly found in your favorite books.

10.2. List the personality traits associated with each character type listed in 10.1.

10.3. Take an outing to a place where people gather. Create a tag for each person you observe and record your observations.

10.4. Think about the community in which you live. What roles do the people in your community play in the day-to-day workings of the community? For example, there may be teachers, ministers, newspaper delivery persons, community leaders, etc. List the traits that make each role uniquely identifiable. The next time you create a character that plays one of these roles, you may be able to use one or more of the traits you've identified here.

EXERCISE 11

11.1. Review the story description and plot outline that you developed in chapter 3. Identify your least developed leading or supporting character. Use the Character Profile Worksheet to further develop that character.

11.2. List the changes the further development of your character has on your story description and plot outline.

11.3. Add any traits that you think should be added to the Character Profile Worksheet.

11.4. Delete any traits that you think should be removed from the Character Profile Worksheet.

EXERCISE 12

12.1. Review your developing story description and plot outline.

12.2. What questions would you like to answer about your characters?

12.3. Use the character type, character profile, or character interview to better define each character and answer those open questions.

12.4. Complete the free-writing exercise for any supporting plots that you introduce.

EXERCISE 13

13.1. Chapter 5 provides the following "What Needs Research" categories: locations and settings, time periods, occupations, medical conditions and legal procedures, customs and cultures, groups and organizations, and family dynamics. Using these categories to stimulate your thinking, identify the research needs in the plot outline and character descriptions that you created for exercise 12.2.

13.2. Now create your personal list of "What Needs Research" categories. This list should include the categories described in chapter 5 and categories you create to fulfill your particular project's needs. Build on this list and keep it for use with future books.

13.3. For each item you've identified as needing research, decide whether the research should be done *before* you begin writing your manuscript or if it can wait until the second or subsequent drafts. Create two lists: one, the "Before" list, with the items needing research before you start writing your book; the other with the items you can follow up on later.

13.4. Chapter 5 provides the following "How to Research" methods: library, interviews, observations, visits, books and videos, Internet, and writing magazines. For each item you've identified as needing research, jot down the research method that you plan to use to obtain the information. Feel free to include research methods not listed here.

13.5. Create your personal "Research Methods" list. This list should include the methods described in chapter 5 and any methods that you identified in 13.3. Build on this list and keep it for use with future books.

13.6. Do your research for the items on your "Before" list.

13.7. After completing your research, update your character descriptions and plot outline to reflect what you've learned.

EXERCISE 14

14.1. Which POV do you see most often in the books you read?

14.2. Select a book scene from a book that's written in first-person POV and answer the following questions:

> **14.2.1.** Who is the POV character?
>
> **14.2.2.** Why do you think that character was chosen as the narrator?
>
> **14.2.3.** What do you learn about the character in the scene?
>
> **14.2.4.** What do you learn about the other characters?

14.3. Select a book scene from a book that's written in limited third-person POV and answer the following questions:

> **14.3.1.** Who is the POV character?
>
> **14.3.2.** Why do you think that character was chosen as the POV character?
>
> **14.3.3.** What do you learn about the POV character in the scene?

14.3.4. What do you learn about the other characters in the scene?

14.3.5. Does the author change POV in the book scene? If so, how many times and are the changes effective?

EXERCISE 15

Write a short passage (two to four sentences) of dialogue for each of the following situations. The first one is done for you.

15.1. Eileen's boss tells her that she's been promoted.
"Congratulations, Eileen," he said, when she reached him. "I know you're going to make your mark with this new job."

15.2. Eileen responds to the news that she's been promoted.

15.3. Rodney accuses his best friend, Derrick, of embezzling money from the company they jointly own.

15.4. Derrick defends himself against Rodney's accusation.

EXERCISE 16

Using dialogue and interior monologue, write a short passage (four to seven sentences) describing the following situations. The first one is done for you.

16.1. Eileen's boss tells her that she's been promoted. POV character: the boss.
Walter watched her walk toward him. Just look at her, he thought. She doesn't deserve this job. Of course, he couldn't say that. No, he had to tow the party line. "Congratulations, Eileen," he said, when she reached him. "I know you're going to make your mark with this new job." She was going to make her mark all right. As far as he was concerned, American productivity was dealt a bad hand when they allowed women in the workplace.

16.2. Eileen after her boss tells her that she's been promoted. POV character: Eileen.

16.3. Jackson sees his high school sweetheart, Patrice, at their twenty-year reunion. POV character: Jackson.

16.4. Patrice sees her high school sweetheart, Jackson, at their twenty-year reunion. POV character: Patrice.

EXERCISE 17

In this exercise you will examine the way your favorite authors weave character information throughout their stories using dialogue, interior monologue, and effective showing and telling.

17.1. Using the Modified Character Profile Worksheet on page 179 identify the character traits the writer reveals about the lead character in the first three chapters of two books you've read recently. When you finish this exercise, look back over the worksheet to see how the information was sprinkled through the three chapters.

EXERCISE 18

18.1. Take your favorite book and identify three action-reaction sequences. Label the components. Remember that all six components don't have to be written explicitly.

>**18.1.1.** Which character is the POV character?

>**18.1.2.** What is this character's goal?

>**18.1.3.** What's keeping the character from attaining the goal?

>**18.1.4.** What do we learn about the POV character in the scene?

>**18.1.5.** What do we learn about the other characters?

18.1.6. What question is left to the reader at the end of the passage?

18.2. In chapters 3 and 4, you began developing a plot outline for your story. Your outline included chapter designations and brief descriptions of the scenes that you planned to include in each chapter. Update your plot outline to reflect the book scenes that you're going to include in each of the first three chapters. For each book scene, indicate the POV character, the place, and the time. If you are unable to outline the three chapters, revisit your characters and do more research. Remember that building the plot outline is a task you'll return to time and again as the pieces of your story take shape.

EXERCISE 19

Visit the fiction section of your local library or bookstore and find three books that you haven't read by authors that you don't usually read. Read the first three chapters of each book and answer the following questions:

19.1. How does each chapter start: with dialogue, interior monologue, showing, telling?

19.2. Does each chapter begin and end with a hook?

19.3. How many book scenes are in each chapter?

19.4. How many pages are in each book scene? in each chapter?

19.5. Do you see any pattern in your answers to questions 19.1–19.4? If so, what is it?

19.6. Which book has the most compelling opening? What makes the opening compelling?

19.7. Which book would you buy? Why?

EXERCISE 20

20.1. If you have completed the plot outline for the first three chapters of your book, write those chapters using the 1-3-100 method. If you can use the method to write your first three chapters, you can use it to write your entire first draft. If you haven't completed the plot outline for those chapters, take some time now to work on it.

20.2. After you finish writing your first three chapters, create a book scene summary table and use it to uncover the revision needs in those chapters. If you can use the summary table to help you uncover revision needs for your first three chapters, you can use it to help you uncover revision needs for your finished manuscript.

20.3. You should keep the Revision Checklist (page 199) handy as you write. You might even consider posting it someplace over your desk. After you have revised your first three chapters, review the checklist again and decide if you want additional topic areas or additional questions. Customizing this list is essential to making it effective in helping you write and revise your manuscript. For example, if you use the word *really* too frequently, you could add an "Overused Words" topic area and include a question to remind yourself to check your use of *really*.